COMPLIANCE LINK

COMPLIANCE LINK

The PricewaterhouseCoopers Regulatory Handbook Series

CROSS-INDEX

1998–1999 Edition

PRICEWATERHOUSECOOPERS

SHARPE PROFESSIONAL
An imprint of M.E. Sharpe, INC.

Copyright © PricewaterhouseCoopers, 1999

All rights reserved. No part of this book may be reproduced in any form without written permission from the publisher, M. E. Sharpe, Inc., 80 Business Park Drive, Armonk, New York 10504

This publication is designed to provide accurate and authoritative information in regard to the subject matter covered. It is sold with the understanding that the publisher is not engaged in rendering legal, accounting, or other professional service. If legal advice or other expert assistance is required, the services of a competent professional person should be sought.

—From the Declaration of Principles jointly adopted by a Committee of the American Bar Association and a Committee of Publishers and Associations

ISBN 0-7656-0271-7
ISSN Pending

Printed in the United States of America

(IPC) 10 9 8 7 6 5 4 3 2 1

COMPLIANCE LINK

Introduction

The Regulatory Handbook Series

The Regulatory Advisory Services practice of **PricewaterhouseCoopers** developed the *Regulatory Handbook* series to provide the firm and its clients with a summary of the primary statutory, regulatory, and judicial principles governing the activities of financial institutions. Each *Handbook* in the series focuses on topics that are the subjects of regulatory examinations by the federal financial institution regulators. We have organized each *Handbook* in a user-friendly manner so that a user will easily find pertinent sections.

Because of the frequency with which the laws and regulations change, we revise each *Handbook* annually. The information in the 1998–1999 edition of the *Handbook* is generally current through January 31, 1998. Check each book to determine its date.

The Compliance Link

This volume, the *Compliance Link*, is a comprehensive index of all six *Regulatory Handbooks*, designed to make a user-friendly tool even more useful. The *Compliance Link* is especially useful in reviewing topics which may be discussed in more than one *Handbook*. For example, three *Regulatory Handbooks* include discussions on the Glass–Steagall Act's restrictions on a financial institution's securities activities and two Handbooks include a discussion of the Currency Transaction Report. The *Compliance Link* will show where to find those references in each *Handbook*. The discussions will be different but, when combined, they will help enhance a financial institution's compliance program.

A Caution about Compliance

Readers should be aware that, although we have highlighted the key legal requirements of the various laws and regulations, compliance remains quite complex, with many technical requirements and frequent—and sometimes varying—agency interpretations. The *Regulatory Handbooks* therefore should be used as only one resource in addition to reviewing the actual statute or regulation, or seeking additional counsel or advice.

An Effective Compliance Program

Each financial institution should have a well-defined and documented Compliance Program. Some of the key elements of an effective program that examiners expect to see include:

1. **Board of directors and senior management involvement** to demonstrate adequate supervision and administration.

2. **An organizational structure** to provide sufficient authority and independence to individuals with compliance responsibilities.

3. **Written policies and procedures** in sufficient detail to assure compliance with all applicable legal requirements.

4. **A training program** to continuously educate personnel on those laws that impact their job responsibilities and on the institution's policies and procedures.

5. The establishment of **internal controls** to provide for and ensure continuing compliance.

6. **A compliance review function** performed by internal or external auditors.

PwC Regulatory Advisory Services

The **PricewaterhouseCoopers** Regulatory Advisory Services practice consists of former senior federal bank regulators, attorneys, and bankers who advise clients on a broad range of U.S. bank regulatory and supervisory issues. The group will assist any financial institution in developing and maintaining an effective compliance program or in evaluating its existing compliance program.

Regulatory Advisory Services also is prepared to conduct reviews of an institution's policies and procedures in a particular area, as well as on-site examinations to assist the institution in evaluating its level of compliance or in preparing for a regulatory exam.

If you wish to receive additional information about the material contained in the *Regulatory Handbooks* or about the compliance services offered by **PricewaterhouseCoopers** Regulatory Advisory Services, please call:

Paul G. Nelson	(202) 414-4331
C. Westbrook Murphy	(202) 414-4301
Gary Welsh	(202) 414-4311
Paul Allan Schott	(202) 822-4272
Kevin Foster	(202) 414-4335
Andrea Conte	(202) 414-4308
Michael VanHuysen	(202) 414-1360
Jeffrey P. Lavine	(202) 414-4320
David R. Sapin	(202) 414-4321

Index

Legend:

COM = *The Commercial Banking Regulatory Handbook*
C   = *The Consumer Banking Regulatory Handbook*
R   = *The Regulatory Reporting Handbook*
RM   = *The Regulatory Risk Management Handbook*
S   = *The Securities Regulatory Handbook*
T   = *The Trust Regulatory Handbook*

A

Absentee guardianship, T22
Abundance of caution, COM175
Abusive behavior, prohibited by debt collectors, C132–33
Access devices, for electronic fund transfer, C80–81
Accountant, independent public (IPA), COM24
Accounting
    collective investment funds (CIFs), T134
    control of, T78–80
    reconcilement in, T80
"Accounting by Creditors for Impairment of a Loan," COM53
Accounting for Certain Investments in Debt and Equity Securities (FASB 115), S30
"Accounting for Mortgage Servicing Rights," COM55
"Accounting for Transfers and Servicing of Financial Assets and Extinguishments of Liabilities," COM51
Accounting standards
    general requirements, COM26
    introduction and purpose, COM22
    laws and regulations references, COM26
    See also Audits and attestation
Adequately capitalized institutions, COM38–39, COM40, COM49, COM71
Adjustable rate mortgage rules
    adjustment notices, C10
    adjustment requirements, C9–10
    disclosure information, C8–9
    introduction and purpose, C8
    laws and regulations references, C10

Adjustable rate mortgage rules *(continued)*
    maximum interest rates, C10
    rate formula or index, C10
    special information booklet, C8
Adjusted add-on amount (Anet), COM65
Adjusted trading, S33
Adjustment notices, C10
Administration
    of collective investment funds (CIFs), T129–34
        accounting, T134
        admission/withdrawal requirements, T131
        audits, T131
        conflict of interest, T132–33
        covered call option funds, T133
        distributions, T131
        fees/expenses for, T132
        financial reports, T131–32, T159
        foreign securities investment funds, T134
        fund management, T130–31
        fund valuation, T131
        good faith mistakes, T132
        index collective investment funds, T134
        investment considerations, T133
        real estate investment funds, T134
        short-term investment funds (STIFs), T133
    of corporate trusts, T52–54
    of estate settlements, T18–19
    of mutual funds, S114–16
    of personal trusts, T24
    of securities lending, S25
    See also Directors
Administrative costs, international loans, COM122
Administrator cum testamento annexo (cta), T18–19
Advance funds, contractual commitment to, COM 136–39
    definition of, COM133
Advanced funds, COM140
    Adverse action, C100
    Adverse changes, notification of, C228

6 Compliance Link

Adverse report, RM35
Advertisement
   brokerage operations, S62
   underwriting/dealing, S94
Advertising, 127
   credit terms, C208
   deposit insurance, C77
   equal credit opportunity, C93
   interest on deposits, C167
   leasing, C62
   nondiscriminatory, C137
   Truth in Savings Act (TISA), C230–31
"Affiliate," definition of, COM10
Affiliate obligations, responsibility for, COM15
Affiliate transactions
   capital percentage limitations, COM12
   collateral requirements, COM12–13
   covered affiliates, COM10, COM14
   covered transactions, COM11, COM14–15
   establishment of control, COM10–11
   exempt affiliates, COM11
   introduction and purpose, COM10
   laws and regulations references, COM16
   purchase from affiliate as underwriter, COM15
   purchase of low-quality assets, COM13
   restrictions
      exemptions to Section 23A, COM13–14
      for savings associations, COM15–16
   restrictions, COM15
Affiliated business arrangements, C178–79
African Development Bank, S17
Age
   and ECOA application processing/evaluation, C95–96
   request for information of, C139
Age Discrimination in Employment Act of 1967, C107
Agency accounts, T22–24
   attorney-in-fact, T24
   custodianship, T23
   escrow agent, T23
   investment advisory agent, T23
   managing agent, T23–24
   safekeeping, T24
Agency fees, international loans, COM123
Aggregate limit, to insiders, COM151
Agreement and Edge corporations, COM110, COM111, COM112–14
   foreign investment activities, COM116–21
   prudential restrictions on, COM115–16
   reserve on deposits (Regulation D), COM192

Agreement Corporations, Edge Act and, C154
Alarm systems, COM32–33
Aliens, TIN not required for, C41–42
Alimony, request for information of, C94
Allocated transfer risk reserve (ATRR), COM121–22
Allowance for loan and lease losses ("ALLL"), COM83
American Exchange's Emerging Company Marketplace, C21
American Institute of Certified Public Accountants (AICPA), RM32, RM34
American Society of Corporate Secretaries, T84
American Stock Exchange (AMSE), C22–23, T60, T66
Amortizing fees, international loans, COM122
Annual fees, disclosure of, C204
Annual percentage rate (APR), C194, C195–96, C212, C213–14
   accuracy tolerances, C196–97
Annual percentage yields (APY), C224, C225, C226–27, C230
Annual Report of Total Deposits and Reservable Liabilities (Form FR 2910a), COM195
Annual Report of Trust Assets, T158–60
Annual reports
   filed with the FDIC, COM22–23
   insider loans and, COM154
Annunzio-Wylie Anti-Money Laundering Act of 1992, C19
Antidiscrimination Rule, C91–92
Application disclosures, C201–2
Applications, nondiscrimination in, C138
Appointment of officers and directors
   affected institutions, COM18
   agency action, COM19
   introduction and purpose, COM18
   laws and regulations references, COM19
   notice requirement, COM18
   waiver of notice requirement, COM19
Appraisal Foundation, COM177
Appraisals, C97–98
   nondiscrimination in, C138
Appraisal Standards Board, COM177
Appraisal Subcommittee of the Federal Financial Institutions Examination Council, COM177
Appraisals. See Real estate appraisals; Real estate ownership
Appraisers. See Real estate appraisals
Assessment, environmental, COM96
Asset control programs. See Foreign asset controls
Asset growth, COM7
Asset quality, COM7
Assets, foreign. See Foreign asset controls

Assumption without lender approval, C171
ATM. *See* Automated teller machines (ATM)
Attorney General, C103
Attorney-in-fact, T24
Audits, S46
    collective investment funds (CIFs), T131
    committee supervision of, T150–51
    committee supervision of reports, T151
    compliance risk and, RM22
    directors and, T12–13
    external
        adverse report, RM35
        board of director responsibility, RM31–32
        certified public accountants (CPAs), T147–49
        competence in, T149
        disclaimer report, RM35
        engagement letters, T149–50
        ethics in, T147–49
        fieldwork standards for, RM33
        general standards for, RM33
        independence in, RM33–34
        independence of, T147–49
        information systems and, RM57
        internal audit coordination, RM30
        qualified report, RM34–35
        report standards for, RM33
        reports for, RM33, RM34–35
        standards for, RM32–33
        unqualified report, RM34
    of fiduciary activities, T150
    internal
        charter for, RM25–26
        compliance function and, RM41–42
        documentation of, RM29
        effectiveness of, T147
        external audit coordination, RM30
        follow-up for, RM29–30
        frequency of, RM26–27
        independence in, RM26, RM55, T144–45
        information systems and, RM55–57
        organization of, RM28
        outsourcing in, RM30–31
        planning of, RM26
        program for, T144–47
        reports for, RM29
        scope of, RM26–27
        supervision of, RM28–29
        work program for, RM27–28
    purpose of, RM22, T144

Audits *(continued)*
    references regarding, RM35, T151
    risk-based, RM18–19, RM20, RM23–25
        policies/procedures for, RM24
        written standards for, RM24–25
    transaction risk and, RM22
Audits and attestation
    annual report, COM22–23
    audit committee, COM24–25
    audited financials, COM23
    environmental, COM96
    general requirements, COM22
    holding company exception, COM25–26
    independent public accountants (IPA), COM24
    introduction and purpose, COM22
    laws and regulations references, COM26
    management report, COM23–24
    See also Accounting standards
Audit system, internal, COM6
Authenticating agent, T52
Automated clearing house (ACH), RM96
    transactions, COM76
Automated teller machines (ATM), RM94
    deposit-taking, C46
    exceptions to funds transfer rules, C35
    and notice of fund availability, C119–20
Available-for-sale securities, S31

B

Balance sheet assets, adjustment for, COM56, COM57–60
Balanced funds, T127
Bank, definition of, C21
Bank Bribery Act, COM28–29
Bank-eligible securities
    Type I, S7, S16, S17, S18, S76
    Type II, S7, S16, S17–18, S76
    Type III, S7, S16, S18, S76
    Type IV, S16, S18, S76
    Type V, S16, S18–19, S76
Bank Enterprise Act (BEA) of 1991
    banking in distressed communities, C13–14
    community development financial institutions fund, C14–16
    introduction and purpose, C12
    laws and regulations references, C16
    lifeline accounts, C12
Bank Enterprise Awards Program, C14, C15–16
Bank holding companies (BHC), RM9
    brokerage operations, S54–55

8 Compliance Link

Bank holding companies (BHC), *(continued)*
   geographic restrictions, RM10
   market risk rule, COM68
   minimum leverage ratio requirements, COM69–70
   mutual funds and, S111–12, S117
   overseas activities, S120, S121, S123–25, S126–127, S129
   and risk-weighted mutual funds, COM60
   securities activities, RM10–11
   and Tier I capital, COM52
   underwriting/dealing, S78, S82
   "well-capitalized," COM73
Bank Holding Company Act, COM145, RM183–84, S8–9, S77
Bank Holding Company Act (BHCA), 8–9
   overseas activities, S120–21
Bank Insurance Fund (BIF), C72, RM6, RM8
Bank powers, brokerage operations, S54
Bank premises, real estate ownership, COM186–87
Bank Protection Act of 1968 (BPA)
   annual report to board, COM33
   introduction and purpose, COM32
   law and regulation references, COM36
   recordkeeping requirements, COM33, COM35
   security issues, COM32–33
   suspicious activity reporting, COM33–36
Bank Secrecy Act, violations of, COM34–35
Bank Secrecy Act (1970), T87–88
   amendment to, C4, C21
   compliance program, C39–40
   currency transaction report (CTR), C19–20
      exemptions, C21–26
   foreign bank account reporting (FBAR), C39
   forfeiture, C37
   funds transfers, C31–35
   institutions subject to, C19
   introduction and purpose, C19
   "know your customer" requirements, C35–36, C37
   laws, regulations, and agency guidelines references, C43–44
   monetary instruments transaction records, C27–28
   other record-keeping requirements, C40–43
   payable through accounts (PTA), C28–29
   registration of nondepository institutions, C43
   structuring of transactions, C30–31
   suspicious transactions, C30
   transportation of currency and monetary instruments (CMIR), C37–38
Bank stock, loans secured by, COM144–45, COM154

Bankers, prohibited conduct of, COM28
Bankers' acceptances, COM139
Banking Act (1933), S6
Banking day, C112, C120
Banking services for employees, Edge corporation, COM114
Bankruptcy, T52
Banks
   capital categories and, COM72–73
   dividends and, COM82–83
   market risk rule, COM68
   minimum leverage ratio requirements, COM69–70
   and risk-weighted mutual funds, COM60
   and Tier I and II capital, COM52
Basis points, more than 75, COM38, COM39
Basle Capital Accord, S79
Basle Committee of Bank Supervisors (Basle Committee), COM49, COM50, COM67
BC, R108
BC (SA), R108
BE-13, R83
BE 605 Bank, R84
Below threshold, COM175
Beneficiary, in funds transfers, C31
Beneficiary's institution, C32
   payment order information (travel rule), C34
Benefit plans. *See* Employee benefit/retirement plans
Best efforts underwriting, S76–77
Best execution, T89, T94
Bilateral netting, S50
BL-1 (SA), R109
BL-2 (SA), R110
BL-3, R111
Blind pooled repurchase agreements, S106
Blocked assets, COM101
Blue sky laws, S13
Board of directors
   and business recovery planning, COM44
   notification of SAR, COM35
Bond registrar, T50
BOPEC composite rating, COM51
BOPEC rating system
   bank condition, RM156–57
   capital adequacy, RM162–65
   consolidated earnings, RM160–62
   finances, RM154
   management, RM154–56
   nonbank condition, RM157–59
   overview of, RM122, RM151–54

BOPEC rating system *(continued)*
    parent company, RM159–60
    risk management, RM165–67
Borrowing, Edge corporation, COM114
BQ-1, R112
BQ-2, R113
Branch-closing notice, C54–55
Branches, bank. *See* Foreign banks; Geographic restrictions
Bribery. *See* Bank Bribery Act
Broker
    definition of, COM39
    notification to FDIC, COM41
Brokerage
    affiliated, T111–12
    directed, T95–96
    placement practices, T9–10
Brokerage operations
    bank holding companies, S54–55
    bank powers, S54
    broker-dealer registration, S56
    confirmation requirements, S67–68
    examinations for, S70–71
    fraud/insider trading, S72–74
    nondeposit investment products, S57
    overview of, S54
    personnel
        policies/procedures, S69
        qualifications/training, S63
        registration, S69–70
        transactions, S73–74
    recordkeeping, S66–67
    references regarding, S56, S65, S71, S74
    retail sales
        advertisement, S62
        compensation, S64
        compliance procedures, S64
        disclosures, S59–61
        mutual fund names, S61–62
        program management, S58
        sales practices, S63–64
        setting for, S62
        third party arrangements, S58–59
    riskless principal transactions, S55
    settlement transactions, S68–69
Brokered deposits, C75
    definition of, COM38
    exceptions and waivers, COM40
    introduction and purpose, COM38

Brokered deposits *(continued)*
    laws and regulations references, COM41
    prohibitions, COM38
Brokers/dealers, special purpose loans to, COM166
Brokers' fees, C167
Business credit, C103
    and signature requirements, C99
Business day, C112
Business loans, C55, C171
    real estate appraisals and, COM175
Business recovery planning (BRP), RM85–91
    board of directors and management responsibilities, COM44
    business impact analysis, RM86
    cold site agreement, RM87
    data file backup, RM88–89
    disk mirroring, RM89
    FFIEC Policy Statement, COM44, COM45
    hot site agreement, RM86–87
    introduction and purpose, COM44
    plan development, RM86, RM90
    plan evaluation, RM86, RM90–91
    planning process, COM45–46
    plan testing, RM86, RM90
    references, COM46
    service bureaus, COM45
    software backup, RM87–88
    strategy options, RM86–87
    telecommunications backup, RM89–90
BXA-621P, R119
BXA-6051P, R119

C

Call Reports, COM12, COM133, COM153, R19–32
    Schedule RC-M, COM190
CAMEL ratings, COM22, COM26
Canada, S17
Capital multiples, COM78
Capital
    definition of, COM51–53, COM133
    PCA categories of, COM38–39, COM49, COM70–72, COM77
    tangible, COM70
    total, COM52
    total leverage, 71t, COM70
    total risk-based, 71t, COM70
    See also Tier I capital; Tier II capital; Tier III capital
Capital adequacy
    derivatives and, S51

Capital adequacy *(continued)*
  introduction and purpose, COM49
  law and regulation references, COM74
  minimum leverage ratio requirement, COM69–70
  prompt corrective action (PCA). *See* Prompt corrective action (PCA)
  risk-based standards
    deductions, COM53–54
    deferred tax assets, COM55–56
    definition of capital, COM51–53
    goodwill, COM54
    introduction, COM50
    qualifying intangible assets, COM54–55
    risk management changes in 1998, COM50–51
    servicing rights, COM55
  risk-weighted assets
    assets sold with recourse, COM60–61
    balance sheet assets, COM56, COM57–60
    calculation of credit equivalent amounts, COM64–66
    credit conversion, COM61–62
    exclusions, COM63
    interest-rate, foreign-exchange, and commodity contracts, COM63, COM66
    interest rate risk (IRR), COM66
    introduction, COM56
    market risk rule, COM67–69
    mutual funds, COM60
    netting, COM64
"Capital Adequacy Guidelines," COM51, COM116
Capital gains, T126–27
Capital limitations test (12 U.S.C. 56), COM82–83
Capital ratios, COM38–39, COM70–71
Capital stock and surplus, definition of, COM12
Capitalization, Edge corporation, COM116
Caps, S39
Carrybacks, COM56
Carryforwards, COM56
Cash accounts, T80–81
Cash overdrafts, T81–82
Cattle, dairy, loans secured by, COM140
CC 7029-06a, R63
CC 7029-06b, R64
CC 7029-07, R63
CC 7610-02, R66
CD-69.4, R116
Cease-and-desist orders, RM179–80
  temporary, RM180
Certificate of deposit (CD), C226, C227

Certified public accountants (CPAs), RM32–35, T147–49
Charitable trust, T20–21
Checking accounts
  demand deposit, C166–67
  lifeline, C12
  See also Expedited Funds Availability Act
Check kiting, C116
Checks, deposit of and fund availability. *See* Expedited Funds Availability Act
Childbearing
  and ECOA application processing/evaluation, C96
  request for information of, C94–95
Child support, request for information of, C94
Chinese Wall concept, S26, S73, T110
CHIPS, C34, RM91
Churning, S94
Citizenship, and ECOA application processing/evaluation, C96–97
Civil liability, Truth in Savings Act (TISA), C231
Civil Rights Act of 1964, Title VII of the, C106–7
Civil Rights Act of 1968, Title VIII of the, C146
Clifford Trust, T20
Closed-end credit
  definition of, C193, C212
  disclosures. *See* Closed-end credit disclosures
  high-rate/high fee mortgages, C217–19
  institution's liability, C222
  mortgages, C219–20
  right of rescission, C220–22
  special foreclosure rules, C221–22
  violation reimbursement, C222
Closed-end credit disclosures, C212
  amount financed, C212, C213
  annual percentage rate (APR), C196, C212, C213–14
  assumption policy information, C216
  creditor's identity, C213
  demand feature information, C214
  finance charge, C197, C212, C213, C221
  high-rate/high fee mortgages, C217–18
  insurance information and debt cancellation, C215–16
  late payment information, C215
  payment schedule, C214
  prepayment information, C214–15
  reference to the credit contract, C216
  required deposit information, C216
  security interest charges, C216
  security interest information, C215
  total of payments, C212, C214
  total sale price, C212, C214

Closed-end investment company, S110
Closing statements, C174
CMIR (Form 4790), R15
Code of Professional Ethics (AICPA), T148–49
Co-fiduciary, T22
Cold site agreement, RM87
Collars, S39
Collateral
　affiliate transactions and, COM12–13
　cash, T98
　margin loans and, COM165–66
　margins, T97–98
　procedures, COM134
　readily marketable, COM133–34
　securities, T98–99
　securities lending, S26–29
Collections and payments, Edge corporation, COM114
Collective investment funds (CIFs)
　administration of, T129–34
　　accounting, T134
　　admission/withdrawal requirements, T131
　　audits, T131
　　conflict of interest in, T132–33
　　covered call option funds, T133
　　distributions, T131
　　fees/expenses for, T132
　　financial reports, T131–32, T159
　　foreign securities investment funds, T134
　　fund management, T130–31
　　fund valuation, T131
　　good faith mistakes, T132
　　index collective investment funds, T134
　　investment considerations, T133–34
　　real estate investment funds, T134
　　short-term investment funds (STIFs), T133
　　written plan for, T130
　advantages of, T126–27
　conversions, T135–36
　disadvantages of, T126–27
　laws/regulations for, T136–41
　proprietary mutual funds, T135
　purpose of, T126–27
　references regarding, T141
　types of
　　corporations/closely related settlors, T129
　　covered call option, T128, T133
　　discretionary, T128
　　diversified/balanced, T127
　　equity, T127

Collective investment funds (CIFs) *(continued)*
　　fixed-income, T128
　　foreign securities investment, T128, T134
　　index collective investment, T128, T134
　　mini-funds, T129
　　mortgage, T128
　　municipal/tax-exempt bond, T128
　　real estate investment, T128, T134
　　short-term investment fund (STIF), T128, T133
　　single loans/obligations, T128–29
　　special exemption, T129
Comaker, C125
Combined rating system, RM148
Commercial Banking Regulatory Handbook, The, C3
Commercial banks, RM6
　geographic restrictions, RM9–10
Commercial paper, discounting of, COM139
Commitment fees, international loans, COM123
Commitments to advance funds, COM136–39
Commodity Futures Trading Commission, C193
Commodity-related contracts, COM63, COM66
Common carrier exemptions (CMFR), C38
Common enterprise, COM134
Common trust funds, T126
Community, management interlocks and, COM158–59
Community Development Financial Institutions Act of 1994, C14
Community Development Financial Institutions Fund, C14–16
Community Development Financial Institutions Program, C14, C15
Community development loans, C56
Community development organization, C14
Community development test, C50, C52–53, C55
Community Enterprise Assessment Credit Board, C13
Community Reinvestment Act (CRA)
　assessment area, C46, C48, C49, C56
　branch-closing notice, C54–55
　community development test, C50, C52–53, C55
　data collection, reporting and disclosure, C46, C55–56, C155
　disclosure statement, C49
　fair lending examinations, C138
　introduction and purpose, C46
　laws and regulations references, C56
　lending, investment, and service tests, C50–52, C55
　performance evaluations, C46, C48, C49–50
　public file maintenance, C46, C48–49
　public notice of, C47–48

Community Reinvestment Act (CRA) *(continued)*
   small-institution performance standards, C50, C53, C55
   statement documenting programs, C46, C47–48
   strategic-plan evaluation, C50, C53–54, C55
Community Reinvestment performance, RM122
Comparable terms, COM15, COM150
Compensation
   brokerage operations, S64
   fees, and benefits, COM7
Competitive Equality Banking Act (1987), COM126, COM127, T111
Compliance. brokerage operations, S64
   See also Environmental assessments
Compliance examination, C4–5, COM3
Compliance function
   Compliance Committee, RM38
   Compliance Officer, RM38
   internal audits and, RM41–42
   operating management
      assistance for, RM41
      oversight of, RM40
      responsibility of, RM40–41
      support for, RM39
   personnel selection, RM42
   personnel training, RM42
      new personnel, RM42–43
      senior management and, RM42
   program goals, RM38
   records
      establishment of, RM43
      review of, RM43–44
   risks, RM18–19
      audits and, RM22
      management of, RM44–45
      sentencing guidelines and, RM190–91
   senior management
      personnel training and, RM42
      responsibility of, RM39–40
      support for, RM38–39
Compliance Link, The, C3
Compliance management, T13
Compliance program, BSA, C39–40
Comprehensive Environmental Response, Compensation and Liability Act (CERCLA) (1980), COM88, COM89, COM90, COM92, T25–26
Comptroller's Handbook for Compliance, The, T154–55
Computer operations, RM67–73
   duty separation/rotation, RM68–69
   equipment control, RM70

Computer operations, *(continued)*
   equipment maintenance, RM69–70
   library control, RM71–72
   operator control, RM71
   rating systems and, RM174
   transaction processing, RM72–73
   workload scheduling, RM70
   See also End-user computing (EUC)
Computer software & systems
   aggregate multiple transactions, C21
   recovery strategies for, COM45–46
"Confession of judgment," C66, C67
Confidentiality, of Suspicious Activity Report (SAR), COM36
Confirmation requirements
   brokerage operations, S67–68
   underwriting/dealing, S91–92
Conflict of interest
   bank directors and, T10
   in bank employee benefit plans, T36
   in collective investment funds (CIFs), T132–33
   in corporate trusts, T53–54
   in external audits, T147–49
   inside information, T10, T110–11
   in portfolio management
      affiliated brokerage, T111–12
      Chinese Wall concept, T110
      conflict transactions, T106–7
      financial benefits, T110–11
      inside information, T110–11
      own-bank/affiliate securities, T108
      related parties/organizations, T109–10
   securities dealer selection, S34
   underwriting/dealing, S84–85, S94–95
Conflict of interests. *See* Related interests
Conservator, T22
Consumer
   definition of, C66
   protection. *See* Right to Financial Privacy Act
Consumer Banking Regulatory Handbook, The, C3
Consumer Compliance Rating System
   composite ratings, RM168–70
   FDIC and, RM170
   overview of, RM122, RM167–68
Consumer Credit Protection Act, C91, C191
Consumer Handbook on Adjustable Rate Mortgages, C8
Consumer Leasing Act
   advertising of lease, C62
   disclosures, C58–62

Index 13

Consumer Leasing Act *(continued)*
   introduction and purpose, C58
   laws and regulations references, C63
   leases covered and not covered, C58
   penalties and liabilities, C63
   record retention, C62
   relation to state law, C62–63
   renegotiations and extensions, C62
Consumer paper, discount of installment, COM140
Consumer reports and reporting agencies. *See* Fair Credit Reporting Act
Contractual commitments, definition of, COM133
Contribution
   definition of, COM170
   political, COM170–71
Controlling interest, definition of, COM149
Control relationships, S94
Conversion agent, T52
Conversion factors, COM61–62, COM64–66
Core capital. *See* Tier I capital
Corporate co-fiduciary, T22
Corporate "know your customer," C36
Corporate trusts
   administration of, T52–54
   authenticating agent, T52
   bankruptcy, T52
   bond indentures, T48–49
   bond registrar, T50
   conversion agent, T52
   debentures, T49
   depository, T51–52
   dividend reinvestment agent, T51
   exchange agent, T52
   fiscal agent, T51
   laws/regulations for, T54–55
   paying agent, T51
   purpose of, T48
   references regarding, T55
   reports on, T159
   stock registrar, T50–51
   stock transfer agent, T49–50
      turnaround performance requirements, T50
   subscription agent, T52
Corporations
   as exempt entities, C22–23
   loans to, COM134
Correspondent banks
   restrictions regarding, COM153–54
   See also Savings associations

Correspondent capital, COM105–7
"Correspondents," COM104
Cosigner, C68–69
   signature requirements, C99
Court-ordered trust, T21
Covered call option funds, T128, T133
Covered calls, S33
Covered securities, T62
Cranston-Gonzalez National Affordable Housing Act, C182
Credit
   extension of. *See* Extension of credit
   securities lending, S26
   See also Equal Credit Opportunity Act
Credit activities, Edge corporation, COM114
Credit cards. *See* Truth in Lending Act (TILA)
Credit conversion factors. *See* Conversion factors
Credit derivatives
   credit default swaps, S40
   credit-linked notes, S41
   risk management for
      counterparty credit, S44
      credit authorization, S47
      monitoring of, S48
      presettlement, S47
      settlement, S47
   total rate of return (TROR) swaps, S40–41
"Credit equivalent amount," COM61, COM64, COM66
Credit exposure, COM64–65
   calculation, COM106–7
Credit history
   and ECOA application processing/evaluation, C96–97
   and signature requirements, C99
Credit Practice Rules
   "cosigner," definition of, C68–69
   "earnings," definition of, C67
   "household goods," definition of, C67
   introduction and purpose, C66
   laws and regulations references, C69
   permitted contract provisions, C66–67
   prohibited contract provisions, C66
   prohibited practices, C68
   transactions covered, C66
Credit reports and reporting agencies. *See* Fair Credit Reporting Act
Credit risk, RM15, RM17, RM19, RM20, RM92–93
Credit scoring system, C95
Credit underwriting, COM6
Credit unions, RM7

Creditor exemption, secured. *See* Secured creditor exemption
Criminal activity, forfeiture and, C37
Criminal Code, C37, C184
Criminal Referral Forms, COM33
Critically undercapitalized institutions, COM49, COM72
CTR (Form 4789), R14
Curator, T22
Currency and monetary instruments, transport of, C37–38
Currency or Monetary Instruments Report (CMIR), T87–88
Currency transaction report (CTR), C22, T87
   aggregation of multiple, C21
   exemptions. *See* Currency transaction report (CTR) exemptions
   filing of, C19, C20, C22
   information required, C20
Currency transaction report (CTR) exemptions, C21–22
   customer exemption statement, C25–26
   determination of an exempt entity, C22–23
   exempt customer list, C26
   general exemptions, C24
   limitations of exemptions, C23
   limited safe harbor, C23
   revocation of exemption, C24
   special exemptions, C24, C25
   unilateral exemptions, C24–25
Current exposure method, COM64–65
Custodianship, T23
Custody
   off-premise, T86
   on-premise, T84–85
Customer
   definition of, C186
   protection. *See* Right to Financial Privacy Act
Customers, prohibited conduct of, COM28
Customs, COM102
Customs Service, C37, C38

D

Dairy cattle, loans secured by, COM140
Data exchange, RM118
Data file backup, RM88–89
Data integrity
   computer virus control, RM84–85
   output control, RM81–82
   telecommunication control, RM82
   transmission control, RM83–84
   user education, RM85

Data security, RM66–67, RM77–78
Database
   administrator for, RM67
   monitoring of, RM67
Daylight overdrafts. *See* Overdrafts, daylight
Dealer, C172
Dealer loans, C172
Debentures, T49
Debt, subordinated, COM53
Debt collection. *See* Fair Debt Collection Practices Act
Debt-for-equity conversions
   FRB approval of, S129
   ownership restrictions, S128–29
Debt-for-equity swaps, COM121
Debt previously contracted (DPC), COM120, COM145
   stock, S19
Declaration of Trust, T126
Deferred tax assets, COM55–56
Defined benefit plans, T32, T33
Defined contribution plans, T32, T33–35
   employee stock ownership (ESOPs), T34
   money purchase, T34
   profit-sharing, T34
   stock bonus, T34
   target benefit, T34
   thrift and savings, T34–35
Delinquency charges, disclosure of (CLA), C60
Demand Deposit Account (DDA), C112, C166–67, T80–81
Demand deposits, COM192
De minimis cap, COM76, COM78–79
Demographic information
   Equal Credit Opportunity Act and, C93–95
   Fair Housing Act and, C139–40
De novo branches, RM10
Department of Commerce
   BE-13, R83
   BE 605 Bank, R84
   BXA-621P, R119
   BXA-6051P, R119
Department of Justice (DOJ), C93, C136
Department of Labor, C106, C108, C109, S28, T37, T38, T112, T121–22, T140
Department of the Treasury, S10
   BC, R108
   BC (SA), R108
   BL-1, R109
   BL-1 (SA), R109
   BL-2, R110
   BL-2 (SA), R110

Department of the Treasury, *(continued)*
   BL-3, R111
   BQ-1, R112
   BQ-2, R113
   FC-1, R76
   FC-2, R77
   FC-3, R78
   Form S, R114
   G-FIN-4, R125
   G-FIN-5, R126
   PD 1025, R51
   SAR, R44–48
Department of Veterans Affairs, C161
Deposit account records, C76
Deposit account requirements, C164–66
Deposit accounts, segregated, loans secured by, COM139
Deposit activities, Edge corporation, COM113–14
Deposit broker
   definition of, COM39
   notification to FDIC, COM41
Deposit insurance
   advertisements of, C77
   categories of ownership, C73–74
   deposits held on another's behalf, C76
   determining legal ownership, C76
   insured deposits, C72
   introduction and purpose, C72
   laws and regulations references, C77
   limit of, C72–73
   official signs requirements, C76–77
   pass-through insurance, C74–76
Deposit insurance assessment credit, C14
Depository, T51–52
Depository Institution Management Interlocks Act, COM158
Depository institutions, definition of, COM192
Depository Institutions Deregulation and Monetary Control Act of 1980, C164
Depository Institutions Deregulation Committee (DIDC), C164
Deposits. *See* Brokered deposits; Reserves on deposits
Deposits, and availability of funds. *See* Expedited Funds Availability Act
Deposits, interest on. *See* Interest on deposits
Deposit slips, and notice of fund availability, C119
Derivatives, T115–17
   capital adequacy and, S51
   caps, S39
   collars, S39

Derivatives, *(continued)*
   counterparty credit risk
      credit authorization, S47
      defined, S44
      management of, S47–48
      monitoring of, S48
      pre-settlement risk, S47
      settlement risk, S47
   credit
      credit default swaps, S40
      credit-linked notes, S41
      total rate of return (TROR) swaps, S40–41
   disclosure for
      in accounting policies footnote, S42
      misleading items, S44
      quantitative/qualitative, S42–43
   disclosure for, S41–44
   floors, S39
   forward contracts, S39
      foreign exchange, S39
      forward rate agreements, S39
   futures contracts, S39
   legal risks, S49–51
      bilateral netting, S50
      multilateral netting, S50
      physical commodity transactions, S50–51
   liquidity risks
      cash flow/funding, S48
      defined, S45
      management of, S48
      market/product, S48
      monitoring of, S48
   market risks
      dealers/active position-takers, S46
      defined, S44
      limited end-users, S46–47
      management of, S46–47
   operation risks
      defined, S45
      documentation, S49
      duty separation, S49
      management of, S49
      personnel quality, S49
      systems quality, S49
      valuation issues, S49
   options, S38
   overview of, S38
   references regarding, S51
   risk management for, S45–51

16 Compliance Link

Derivatives, *(continued)*
  senior management supervision
    audit coverage, S46
    risk responsibility, S45–46
    risk systems, S46
    written policies/procedures, S45
  settlement risks, S47
  swaps, S38, S40–41
"Designation of Exempt Person," C22
Director
  definition of, COM148
  See also Board of directors
Directors
  audits and, T12–13
  compliance management, T13
  discharging duties, T8–9
  internal controls and, T13
  policies/procedures regarding
    brokerage placement, T9–10
    conflict of interest, T10
    inside information, T10
    investments, T9
    personnel, T10–12
    service pricing, T11–12
  proxy voting and, T12
  purpose of, T8
  recordkeeping and, T12
  references regarding, T13
  risk management and, T13
Disaster planning. *See* Business recovery planning
Disclaimer report, RM35
Disclosure, public, COM153
Disclosures
  for brokerage operations, S59–61
  for derivatives
    in accounting policies footnote, S42
    misleading items, S44
    quantitative/qualitative, S42–43
Disclosure statement, ARM, C8–9
Discretionary funds, T128
Discrimination. *See* Equal Credit Opportunity Act (ECOA); Equal Employment Opportunity Act; Fair Housing Act
Disk mirroring, RM89
Disparate impact, C92–93
Disparate treatment, C92
Distressed communities, C13–14
Diversified funds, T127
Dividend/income claims, T83
Dividend reinvestment agent, T51

Dividends
  introduction and purpose, COM82
  laws and regulations references, COM86
  limitations for banks
    capital limitations, COM82–83
    earnings limitations, COM82, COM83
    "surplus surplus" transfers, COM83
  limitations for savings associations
    OTS future revision, COM84
    OTS regulations and future revision, COM84
    OTS supervision restrictions, COM85–86
    OTS tier dividends, COM84–85
    OTS tier levels, COM84
Document imaging, RM106
Documentation
  information systems
    manual documentation, RM66
    program documentation, RM61, RM65–66
  internal audits, RM29
  regulatory examination, RM50
Documents of title, loans secured by, COM139
Domestic branches, Edge corporations, COM113
Dow Jones Industrials, T128
Dual control procedures, T85
Dual licensing system, RM11
Duty separation, S49, T85
Dwelling, definition of, C136, C155

E

Early termination, disclosure of (CLA), C60
Earnings, COM7
  assignment of, C66, C67
  definition of, C67
Earnings limitations test (12 U.S.C. 60), COM82, COM83
Eavesdropping, RM83
Economic sanctions. *See* Foreign asset controls
"Edgar," C23
Edge Act and Agreement Corporations, C154, RM11
Edge and Agreement Corporations, COM110, COM111, COM112–14, S121, S123–25, S126
  foreign investment activities, COM116–21
  prudential restrictions on, COM115–16
  reserve on deposits (Regulation D), COM192
Elections, COM170
Electronic Data Processing (EDP) Examination Handbook, The, COM46
Electronic Fund Transfer Act (EFTA) of 1978, C35
  consumer liability, C86–87
  disclosures, C81–84

Electronic Fund Transfer Act (EFTA) *(continued)*
   error resolution procedures, C84–86
   introduction and purpose, C80
   issuance of access devices, C80–81
   laws and regulations references, C88
   notification of unauthorized transfer, C87–88
   transactions covered and not covered, C80
Electronic funds transfer (EFT), C80
   automated clearinghouse (ACH), RM96
   automated teller machines (ATMs), RM94
   communication control, RM94
   credit risk, RM92–93
   insurance for, RM100–101
   internal control, RM98–101
   internet banking, RM97–98
   nondeposit investment products, RM98
   operational control, RM93
   payment order origination, RM91–92
   PINs, RM95, RM98–100
   point-of-sale (POS), RM94–95
   retail, RM94, RM98–101
   risk control, RM92
   smart cards, RM95
   wholesale, RM91
"Eligible country," COM121
Emergency conditions, and funds availability, C116–17
Emergency planning. *See* Business recovery planning
Employee benefit/retirement plans
   benefit plans, T32
   defined benefit plans, T32, T33
   defined contribution plans, T32, T33–35
      employee stock ownership (ESOPs), T34
      money purchase, T34
      profit-sharing, T34
      stock bonus, T34
      target benefit, T34
      thrift and savings, T34–35
   FDIC insurance for, T44–45
   Individual retirement accounts (IRAs), T32, T35–36, T44–45
   laws/regulations for, T32–33, T36–44
   pension plans, T32–35
   purpose of, T32
   references regarding, T45
   self-administered bank employee, T36–37
   self-employed retirement trusts, T35
Employee Retirement Income Security Act (ERISA) (1974), S28, T32–33, T36–44
   directed brokerage, T95–96

Employee Retirement Income Security Act *(continued)*
   fiduciary liability, T39–40
   fiduciary responsibility, T38, T39
      exceptions to, T38–39
   objective of, T37–38
   participant loans, T42–43
   party-in-interest transactions, T40–42, T112, T140
      restriction exemptions, T121–22, T140
   percent limitation, T40–41
   prohibited transactions, T40
      exemptions to, T41–44
   prudent person rule, T105–6
   securities lending, T98
   violation referral, T38
Employee stock ownership plans (ESOPs), T34
Employee training, Expedited Funds Availability Act and, C121
Employees, banking services for, COM114
Employer-employee referral fee exemption, C177–78
Employment
   denial of based on a consumer report, C127
   See also Equal Employment Opportunity Act
"Ending balance" method, C229
End-user computing (EUC)
   acquisition criteria, RM102
   communications in, RM105–6
   development of, RM103–4
   existing inventory, RM101–2
   security for, RM102–3
   usage of, RM104–5
Engagement letters, T149–50
Entities, determination of exempt, C22–23
Entities exercising governmental authority, C21
Environmental assessments, COM96
   fiduciary liabilities, limitations on, COM92–93
   hazards, COM88–89
   introduction and purpose, COM88
   laws and regulations references, COM97
   liabilities, COM89
   risk program, COM95–97
   secured creditor exemption, COM89, COM90–92
      for underground storage tanks (USTs), COM90, COM93–95
Environmental audit, COM96
Environmental compliance activities, permissible, secured creditor exemption for UST, COM94–95
Environmental laws
   for corporate trusts, T54
   for personal trusts, T25–27

Environmental Protection Agency (EPA), COM88, COM90
Environmental review, COM96
Environmental risk analysis, COM96
Environmental risk program, COM95–97
Equal Credit Opportunity Act (ECOA)
- advertising, C93
- agency referrals, C103
- application processing and evaluation, C95–97, C100–101
- applications and information gathering, C93–95
- appraisals, C97–98
- business credit exceptions, C103
- corrective action, C104
- credit extension, C98–100
- fair lending examinations, C138
- furnishing credit information, C101
- general antidiscrimination rule, C91–92
- government monitoring information, C102
- indirect lending disclosure, C102
- introduction and purpose, C91
- laws and regulations references, C104
- loans covered by, C91
- notification, C100–101
- penalties, C104
- prequalification and preapproval programs, C101
- record retention, C102
- types of lending discrimination, C92–93

Equal Employment Opportunity Act
- Age Discrimination in Employment Act of 1967, C107
- agency guidance, C106
- Equal Pay Act of 1963, C107–8
- Executive Orders No. 11141 & No. 11246, C108–9
- introduction and purpose, C106
- laws and regulations references, C109–10
- Rehabilitation Act of 1973, C109
- summary of laws and regulations, C106
- Title VII of the Civil Rights Act of 1964, C106–7
- Vietnam Era Veterans Readjustment Act of 1974, C109

Equal Employment Opportunity Commission (EEOC), C106
"Equal Housing Lender" logo & poster, C137, C139
Equal Pay Act of 1963, C107–8
Equity derivative-related contracts, COM63–64
Equity funds, T127
Equity investments, S19, S20
Error resolution procedures
- credit card billing, C207–8
- electronic fund transfers, C84–86
- Real Estate Settlement Procedures Act, C181

Escrow statements, C176–77
- of flood insurance payments, C149
Escrow accounts, C175–76
Escrow agent, T23
Estate settlements
- administrator, T18
- administrator cum testamento annexo (cta), T18–19
- executor, T18
Ethics. *See* Conflict of interest
Eurocurrency liabilities, COM192, COM193, COM195
Examinations, brokerage operations, S70–71
Exchange agent
- for corporate trusts, T52
- for shareholder services, T70
Exchange rate-related contracts, COM63, COM66
Executive officers
- definition of, COM149
- filing of FFIEC 004, COM154
- loan restrictions for, COM152, COM154–55
Executive Orders No. 11141 & No. 11246, C108–9
Executors, T18
Exempt entities, determination of, C22–23
Expedited Funds Availability Act
- $100 rule, C113–14
- amendment to, C4
- availability of exception deposits, C118
- check collection, C121
- covered accounts, C112
- disclosures, C118–20
- employee training, C121
- exception notice, C117–18
- interest payments, C229
- introduction and purpose, C112
- laws and regulations references, C121
- local and nonlocal checks, C114
- next-day availability, C113
- overdrafts, C115
- payment of interest, C118
- reasonable cause to doubt collectibility, C115–17
- record retention, C120–21
- redeposited checks, C115
- safeguard exceptions, C114–17
- when funds are considered deposited, C120
Expenditure, definition of, COM170
Exposure limits, interbank liabilities and, COM105
Extension of credit
- definition of, COM150
- to insiders. *See* Insiders, loans to
- *See also* Lending limits

F

Fair Credit Reporting Act (FCRA)
    consumer reporting agencies, C124, C125–26
    coverage, C124
    denial of employment, C127
    disclosures, C124–25
    introduction and purpose, C124
    laws and regulations references, C127
    penalties and liabilities, C127
    prescreening, C126–27
    transactions not covered, C124
Fair Debt Collection Practices Act
    activities covered and not covered, C130
    communications with consumers, C130–31
    communications with third parties, C131–32
    deceptive forms, C134
    introduction and purpose, C130
    legal actions by debt collectors, C134
    legal reference, C134
    multiple debts, C134
    prohibited practices, C132–34
    validation of debts, C132
Fair Housing Act
    activities covered, C136
    equal housing lender logo & poster, C137, C139
    Fair Housing Home Loan Data System, C140–41
    fair lending examinations, C138–39
    introduction and purpose, C136
    laws and regulations references, C141
    loan application register reporting, C140
    monitoring information, C139–40
    prohibited discriminatory practices, C136–38
Fair Housing Home Loan Data System (FHHLDS), C140–41
Fair lending examinations, C138–39
Fair Lending Guidance: Responsibilities and Timeframes, C139
Fair practice standards, underwriting/dealing, S92–94
Farmers Home Administration (FmHA), C155
Farm loans, small, C55
FAS 109, COM55
FAS 114, COM53
FAS 115, COM54
FAS 122, COM55
FAS 125, COM51
FBAR (TD F90-22-1), R16
FC-1, R76
FC-2, R77

FC-3, R78
FDIC 6420/24, R85
FDIC 8020/05, R60
Federal agency, loans guaranteed by, COM139
Federal Deposit Insurance Act, COM6, S9, S20, S120
    Section 36, COM22
Federal Deposit Insurance Corporation (FDIC), C12, S9, S20
    annual reports filed with, COM22–23
    audits and accounting standards, COM22
    balance sheet assets, COM58
    brokerage operations, S55, S57, S59, S60–61, S62, S66, S68, S70
    brokered deposits, COM38, COM40
    capital adequacy, COM49, COM52
    deposit brokers, COM41
    dividends and, COM82
    employee benefit/retirement plans, T44–45
    FDIC 6420/24, R85
    FDIC 8020/05, R60
    federal/state regulations and, RM11–12
    foreign operations, COM110
    government securities, T86
    Interlocks Act, COM158
    international trust services, T74
    management interlocks, COM160
    mutual funds and, S114
    overseas activities, S120
    personal trusts, T28
    pledge requirements, T82
    Prompt Corrective Action (PCA), T44–45
    rating systems and, RM125, RM136–37, RM146, RM170, RM175
    real estate lending standards, COM180
    regulatory enforcement and, RM184–86
    regulatory examination and, RM48
    regulatory system and, RM6, RM7, RM8, RM11–12
    risk-focused examination and, RM16–17
    underwriting/dealing, S76, S84–85, S99, S101–2, S105
Federal Deposit Insurance Corporation Improvement Act (FDICIA) (1991), C54, RM22, RM55, S9, S17, S20, S50, T44–45
    brokered deposit restrictions, COM38
    loans to insiders, COM148
    Section 121, COM26
Federal Election Campaign Act, COM170
Federal Emergency Management Agency (FEMA), C144, C146, C148, C149, C150
    FEMA Form 81-93, R42

Federal Energy Regulatory Commission (FERC), T27
Federal Financial Institutions' Examination Council (FFIEC), C154, C157, RM48, RM122, RM125–26, RM145–46, RM167–68
    Appraisal Subcommittee, COM177
    FAS 122, COM55
    FFIEC 001, R134
    FFIEC 002, R86–87
    FFIEC 002S, R88
    FFIEC 004, R62
    FFIEC 006, R136
    FFIEC 009, R67
    FFIEC 009a, R67
    FFIEC 019, R89
    FFIEC 030, R32, R68
    FFIEC 031, R20, R21, R22, R26
    FFIEC 032, R20, R21, R22
    FFIEC 033, R20, R21
    FFIEC 034, R20, R21, R22, R23
    FFIEC 035, R79
    Fiduciary Activities Special Report, R135
    Policy Statement on business recovery planning, COM44, COM45
    repurchase agreements, S22–23
    securities lending, S24–25
Federal Home Loan Bank, C24, C113, C118
Federal Home Loan Bank Board, RM17, RM125–26
Federal Home Loan Banks, COM194
Federal Home Loan Mortgage Corporation (FHLMC), C155
Federal Housing Administration (FHA), C155, C161
    loan prepayment disclosures, C182
    mortgage, C182
Federal Housing Authority, C145
Federally chartered institutions, COM170
Federal National Mortgage Association (FNMA), C155
Federal National Mortgage Corporation, COM188
Federal office, definition of, COM170
Federal regulations, RM11–12
Federal Reserve
    balance sheet assets, COM58
    capital adequacy, COM49, COM52–53
    CD-69.4, R116
    daylight overdrafts. *See* Overdrafts, daylight
    dividends, COM83
    FR 20, R93
    FR 20a, R59, R93
    FR 2000, R54
    FR 2001, R54
    FR 2006, R117

Federal Reserve *(continued)*
    FR 2050, R69
    FR 2064, R70
    FR 2068, R90
    FR 2069, R91
    FR 2225, R92
    FR 2314, R71
    FR 2415, R122
    FR 2416, R36
    FR 2502q, R72
    FR 2644, R37
    FR 2886b, R118
    FR 2900, R55–56
    FR 2900q, R55–56
    FR 2910a, R57
    FR 2910q, R58
    FR 2915, R80
    FR 2950, R73
    FR 2951, R94
    FR 4002, R97
    FR Y-6, R100
    FR Y-6A, R101
    FR Y-7, R95
    FR Y-8, R102
    FR Y-8f, R96
    FR Y-9C, R103
    FR Y-9LP, R103
    FR Y-9SP, R103
    FR Y-11I, R104
    FR Y-11Q, R105
    FR Y-20, R106
    G-FIN, R124
    G-FINW, R127
    HMDA-LAR, R40–41
    intangible assets, COM55
    interbank liabilities, COM104–7
    Interlocks Act, COM158, COM159, COM160
    international banking operations, COM110–24
    loans to insiders, COM148
    margin loans, COM164–67
    MSD, R128
    MSD-4, R129
    MSD-5, R130
    MSDW, R131
    overdrafts. *See* Overdrafts, daylight
    Policy Statement, COM76
    real estate lending standards, COM180
    reserves on deposits, COM192–95 (passim)
    Tier I leverage ratio, COM51

Federal Reserve *(continued)*
   tying provisions, COM199
   "well-capitalized" category for BHCs, COM73
Federal Reserve Act, S10, S78, S81, S82, S85, S120, S123
   reserves on deposits, COM195
   Section 22(g), COM148
   Section 22(h), COM148
   Section 23A, COM10–11, COM13–14, COM15–16
   Section 23B, COM10, COM14–16
   Section 25(a), COM113
Federal Reserve Bank, COM145, COM194, S81–82, S83
Federal Reserve Bank Stock, balance sheet assets, COM58
Federal Reserve Banks, C24, C113, C118, RM9, RM92, RM96
Federal Reserve Board, C12
   Bank Holding Company Act (BHCA) and, S8–9, S77, S120–21
   brokerage operations, S54–55, S62, S66, S70, S74
   credit practices, C66
   equal credit opportunity, C91
   finance charge tolerances, C197
   free-riding, T93–94
   Glass-Steagall Act and, S7, S8
   home equity brochure, C209
   home mortgage disclosure, C154
   Home Ownership and Equity Protection Act of 1994, C217, C219
   interest on deposits, C164
   investment activities, S20, S29
   model reverse mortgage disclosure form, C220
   mutual funds and, S111, S113, S114–15, S117
   overseas activities, S120, S121, S122, S123, S124, S125, S126–29
   portfolio management, T116–17
   proprietary mutual funds, T135
   rating systems and, RM125, RM146, RM149–50, RM151–54, RM175
   real estate settlement procedures, C173
   regulatory examination and, RM48, T154
   regulatory system and, RM8–9, RM11
   right to financial privacy, C187
   risk-focused examination and, RM16
   truth in savings, C224, C226–27, C228, C229
   underwriting/dealing, S76, S77–83, S99, S101–2
   year 2000 problem, RM110–12
   See also under Regulations B through Z
Federal Reserve System, COM76, S6, S10
   audits and, RM30–31
   regulatory system and, RM8–9, RM11

Federal Rules of Civil or Criminal Procedure, C185
Federal Trade Commission (FTC), C66
Federal Trade Commission Act, C66
Fedwire, C80, COM76, COM79, COM80, RM91
   payment order information and, C33–34
   payment system risk and, COM76
Fee appraisers, COM178
Fee mortgages, high-rate/high, C217–19
Fees
   annual percentage rate (APR), C195–96
   disclosure of, C61, C197–99, C204
   finders' and brokers, C167
   referral, and kickbacks, C177–78
   for required statements, C179
FEMA Form 81-93, R42
FFIEC 001, R134
FFIEC 002, R86–87
FFIEC 002S, R88
FFIEC 004, COM154, R62
FFIEC 006, R136
FFIEC 009, R67
FFIEC 009a, R67
FFIEC 019, R89
FFIEC 030, R32, R68
FFIEC 031, R20, R21, R22, R26
FFIEC 032, R20, R21, R22
FFIEC 033, R20, R21
FFIEC 034, R20, R21, R22, R23
FFIEC 035, R79
FFIEC Electronic Data Processing (EDP) Examination Handbook, The, COM46
FHA. *See* Federal Housing Administration (FHA)
Fiduciary, real estate appraisals and, COM176
Fiduciary Activities-Special Report, R135
Fiduciary and investment advisory activities, Edge corporation, COM114
Fiduciary liabilities, limitations on, COM92–93
Fiduciary purchase, COM15
"Fiduciary Risk Management of Derivatives and Mortgage-Backed Securities" (1996), T115–16
Final rule exemptions, C21
Finance charge, C193, C194, C196, C197–200
Finance charge tolerances, C195, C197, C221
Finance leases, COM128–29, COM187
Financial Accounting Standards Board (FASB), RM32, S30
Financial advisory relationships, S94–95
Financial Crimes Enforcement Network (FinCen), C22, C24, COM36
Financial institution responsibilities, C38

Financial institutions, loans to, COM139
Financial privacy. *See* Right to Financial Privacy Act (RFPA)
Financials statements, audited, COM23
Finders, securities lending, S27–28
Fingerprinting, employee, T67
Firm commitment underwriting, S76
FIRREA
   brokered deposit restrictions, COM38
   dividend restrictions, COM82
   management interlocks, COM158
   Section 914, COM18
First Day Letter, RM49
Fiscal agent, T51
Fixed-income funds, T128
Fixed-term (certificate) account, C164–65
Flood Disaster Protection Act of 1973 (FDPA)
   community requirements, C147
   insurance coverage, C147
   introduction and purpose, C144
   laws and regulations references, C151
   loans covered, C145–46
   mandatory flood insurance, C145
   mortgage portfolio protection plan (MPPP), C149–50
   National Flood Insurance Programs (NFIP), C144–45, C146, C147
   notification requirements, C147–49
   penalties, C150–52
   record-keeping requirements, C150–51
   regulatory requirements, C145
Flood Hazard and Boundary Maps, C144
Flood Insurance Rate Maps, C144
Floors, S39
FOCUS reports, S81
Foreclosure
   postforeclosure and secured creditor exemption, COM91–92
   preforeclosure and secured creditor exemption, COM90–91
   rules, C221–22
   underground storage tanks (USTs) and, COM95
Foreign asset controls
   blocked assets, registration of, COM101
   countries subject to, COM100
   introduction and purpose, COM100
   laws and regulations references, COM102
   penalties, COM102
   reporting of transfers, COM102
   scope of, COM100–101
   specially designated persons and entities, COM101

Foreign bank account reporting (FBAR), C39
Foreign bank accounts, C28
Foreign banking operations. *See* International banking operations
Foreign Bank Supervision Enhancement Act (1991), RM146
Foreign banks
   rating systems
   daylight overdrafts, COM80
   payment orders and, C31–32
      annual examination plan, RM150–51
      Combined rating, RM148
      ROCA, RM122, RM146–48, RM150
      SOSA, RM122, RM149–50
   regulatory enforcement, RM186–87
Foreign branches of U.S. banking institutions, COM110–12
Foreign Corrupt Practices Act (1977), T74
Foreign exchange, Edge corporation, COM114
Foreign exchange contracts, COM63, COM66
Foreign exchange risk, RM15
Foreign financial institutions, C38
Foreign governments, loans to, COM135
Foreign investments, Edge and Agreement corporation, COM116–21
Foreign joint venture, COM117
Foreign portfolio investments, COM116, COM117
Foreign securities investment funds, T128, T134
Foreign subsidiary, COM117
Forfeiture law, Bank Secrecy Act and, C37
Form 10-K, C23
Form 81-93, C146
Form 144, T119
Form 851, C23
Form 926, T75
Form 1065, T140
Form 4789, T87
Form 4790, C37, T87
Form FR2900, COM194, COM195
Form FR 2910a, COM195
Form FR 2910q, COM194
Form FR 2950/2951, COM195
Form G-36(OS), S97
Form G-FIN, S99–100, S102
Form G-FIN-4, S100, S102
Form G-FIN-5, S100, S102
Form G-FIN-W, S102
Form MSD, S86
Form MSD-4, S88, S100

Index 23

Form MSD-5, S88
Form S, R114
Form TA-1, S116, T62
Form TA-2, T70
Form TDF 90-22.1, C39
Form U-1, COM164–65
Form U-4, S100
Form X-17F-1A, T67
Forward-collection test, C121
Forward contracts, S39, T123–24
    foreign exchange, S39
    forward rate agreements, S39
457 Plan, C74
FR 20, R93
FR 20a, R59, R93
FR 2000, R54
FR 2001, R54
FR 2006, R117
FR 2050, R69
FR 2064, R70
FR 2068, R90
FR 2069, R91
FR 2225, R92
FR 2314, R71
FR 2315, R122
FR 2415, R122
FR 2416, R36
FR 2502q, R72
FR 2644, R37
FR 2886b, R118
FR 2900, R55–56
FR 2900q, R55–56
FR 2910a, R57
FR 2910q, R58
FR 2915, R80
FR 2930, R93
FR 2950, R73
FR 2951, R94
FR 4002, R97
Free-ride period, C203
Free-riding, T93–94
Free trade zone, COM124
FR Y-6, R100
FR Y-6A, R101
FR Y-6a, R101
FR Y-7, R95
FR Y-8, R102
FR Y-8f, R96
FR Y-9C, R103

FR Y-9LP, R103
FR Y-9SP, R103
FR Y-11I, R104
FR Y-11Q, R105
FR Y-20, R106
FR Y-20 reports, S81
FSLIC Resolution Fund, COM58, COM59
Full-payout leases, COM127–28
Funds transfer rules
    exceptions to, C35
    information retrieval and, C34–35
    international, C32
    overview of, C31
    parties involved in, C31–32
    payment orders and, C31, C33–35
    record-keeping requirements, C32, C34
Futures contracts, S39

G

Gains trading, S32
Garnishment, credit practice rules and, C67
Gender, request for information of, C94, C139
General Accounting Office (GAO), C185
Generally accepted accounting principles (GAAP), RM32, RM34–35
    audited financials, COM23
    general accounting standards, COM26
    other real estate owned (OREO), COM188, COM190
Generally accepted auditing standards (GAAS), RM32–33, RM34–35
Geographic restrictions
    bank holding companies, RM10
    commercial banks, RM9–10
    de novo branches, RM10
    Interstate Act (1994), RM9–10
    opting-out, RM9–10
    savings associations, RM10
G-FIN, R124
G-FIN-4, R125
G-FIN-5, R126
G-FINW, R127
Gifts to minors, deposit insurance coverage for, C74
Glass-Steagall Act (1933), RM10, T135, T139
    equity investments and, S19
    overview of, S6
    Section 16, S6-7, S10, S54, S76, S85, S111
    Section 20, S6, S7, S8, S18, S19, S76–84, S114–15, S126
    Section 21, S6, S7-8, S76, S111

Glass-Steagall Act (1933) *(continued)*
   Section 32, S6, S8
   underwriting/dealing and, S6-8, S18, S19, S76–84
Gold bullion, COM58
Good faith, COM164–65
Good faith estimate of settlement costs, C173–74
Goodwill, COM54
Governmental entities, exempt, C22
Government real estate transactions, COM175–76
Government Securities Act (GSA) (1986), T86–87
   broker-dealer registration, S99–100
   exemptions, S100–101
   hold-in-custody repurchase agreements, S23, S104–6
   overview of, S10, S99
   recordkeeping requirements, S101–2
   safekeeping requirements, S102–4
   securities sales practices, S106–8
Great Depression, S6
Grey lists, S73
Gross current exposure (NGR), COM65
Group trusts, T126
G.S.E., COM175–76
Guarantees, disclosure of (CLA), C60
Guarantor, C125
Guardianship, T22
Guide to the Federal Reserve's Payments System Risk Policy, The, COM77

H

Harassment, prohibited by debt collectors, C132–33
Harvard College v. Amory, T105
Hazards, environmental. *See* Environmental assessments
Held-to-maturity securities, S30
High-rate/high fee mortgages, C217–19
HMDA-LAR, R40–41
Hold-in-custody repurchase agreements, S23, S104–6
Home equity lines of credit (HELCs), C156, C172, C209–12
Home equity loans, C174
Home Mortgage Disclosure Act (HMDA)
   amendment to, C4
   data accuracy, C156
   data reporting under Community Reinvestment Act, C46, C55–56, C155
   disclosure statement, C49, C56, C157
   Fair Housing Act and, C138, C140–41
   home equity lines of credit, C156
   home mortgage loans, C56
   introduction and purpose, C154

Home Mortgage Disclosure Act *(continued)*
   laws and regulations references, C157
   Loan/Application Register, C141, C156
   loans covered and excluded, C155
   nondepository mortgage lenders, C154
   public notice, C157
   submission of register, C157
Home Owner's Loan Act (HOLA), COM128, COM160, S9, S10
Home Ownership and Equity Protection Act of 1994, C217, C219
Home-ownership counseling, C160–61
Hot site agreement, RM86–87
"Household goods," definition of, C67
Housing and Urban Development (HUD). *See* U.S. Department of Housing and Urban Development (HUD)
HR-10 trusts, T35, T137
HUD. *See* U.S. Department of Housing and Urban Development (HUD)

I

Identification
   creditor's, C213
   personal identification number (PIN), C201
   of person receiving benefits, C179
   taxpayer identification number (TIN), C41–42
   transaction, C204–5
Income, and ECOA application processing/evaluation, C96
Incompetent guardianship, T22
Indemnification, S28–29
Independence (audits)
   external, RM33–34
   internal, RM26, RM55
Independent public accountants (IPA), COM24
Index collective investment funds, T128, T134
Individual ownership accounts, C73
Individual retirement accounts (IRAs), C74, C165, T32, T35–36, T44–45, T137, T138, T159
Information control, RM51
Information systems
   business recovery planning (BRP), RM85–91
      business impact analysis, RM86
      cold site agreement, RM87
      data file backup, RM88–89
      disk mirroring, RM89
      hot site agreement, RM86–87
      plan development, RM86, RM90

Information systems *(continued)*
    plan evaluation, RM86, RM90–91
    plan testing, RM86, RM90
    software backup, RM87–88
    strategy options, RM86–87
    telecommunications backup, RM89–90
  computer operations, RM67–73
    duty separation/rotation, RM68–69
    equipment control, RM70
    equipment maintenance, RM69–70
    library control, RM71–72
    operator control, RM71
    transaction processing, RM72–73
    workload scheduling, RM70
  data integrity
    computer virus control, RM84–85
    output control, RM81–82
    telecommunication control, RM82
    transmission control, RM83–84
    user education, RM85
  development/programming, RM60–67
    database administrator, RM67
    database monitoring, RM67
    data security, RM66–67
    development standards, RM61–62
    manual documentation, RM66
    program documentation, RM61, RM65–66
    programming personnel, RM64–65
    program modification, RM64
    program security, RM65
    program testing, RM63
    project control, RM61
    software implementation, RM63
    software selection, RM62
    system development life cycle (SDLC), RM62
  document imaging, RM106
  electronic funds transfer (EFT)
    automated clearing house (ACH), RM96
    automated teller machines (ATMs), RM94
    communication control, RM94
    credit risk, RM92–93
    insurance for, RM100–101
    internal control, RM98–101
    internet banking, RM97–98
    nondeposit investment products, RM98
    operational control, RM93
    payment order origination, RM91–92
    PINs, RM95, RM98–100
    point-of-sale (POS), RM94–95

Information systems *(continued)*
    retail, RM94, RM98–101
    risk control, RM92
    smart cards, RM95
    wholesale, RM91
  end-user computing (EUC)
    acquisition criteria, RM102
    communications in, RM105–6
    development of, RM103–4
    existing inventory, RM101–2
    security for, RM102–3
    usage of, RM104–5
  external audits, RM57
  internal audits
    application development/testing, RM56–57
    auditor role, RM55–56
    frequency of, RM56
    independent, RM55
    scope of, RM56
  management of
    insurance coverage, RM59–60
    internal control, RM58–59
    organization, RM57–58
    outsourcing arrangements, RM60
    planning, RM58
    policies/procedures, RM58
    reports, RM59
    technology, RM60
  overview of, RM54
  references regarding, RM107
  security
    administration of, RM74–75
    building protection, RM76
    computer protection, RM76–77
    contingency planning, RM76
    data protection, RM77–78
    logical access control, RM78–79
    network protection, RM76–77
    plan for, RM75–76
    principles of, RM73–74
    provisions of, RM74
    system logs, RM79–81
    unauthorized disclosures, RM81
Inside information, S11, S26, S72–74, T10, T110–11
Insider Trading and Securities Fraud Enforcement Act (1988), S11, S72–73, T110
Insiders
  annual reports, COM154
  correspondent bank restrictions, COM153–54

Insiders *(continued)*
    definitions, COM148–50
    disclosures by banks, COM153
    executive officer restrictions and reports, COM152, COM154–55
    introduction and purpose, COM148
    laws and regulations references, COM155
    loans secured by stock reports, COM154
    maintenance of records, COM153
    prohibitions, COM150–52
    reports by banks, COM153
    savings associations restrictions, COM154–55
Institutional Delivery System, T96
Insurance. *See* Federal Deposit Insurance Corporation (FDIC); *See* specific insurances
    ECOA and, C99–100
    See also Deposit insurance; Flood Disaster Protection Act of 1973 (FDPA)
Insurance
Insurance payments, C60
Insured deposits. *See* Deposit insurance
Intangible assets, deduction of, COM54–55
Interagency Guidelines Establishing Standards for Safety and Soundness, (1995), COM6
    agencies' existing authority, COM7, RM195
    asset quality and earnings standards, COM6, COM7
    compliance plan, COM7–8
    compliance plan requirement, RM195–96
    enforcement of, RM196
    enforcement, COM8
    introduction and purpose, COM6
    operational and managerial standards, COM6–7, RM-194–95
    regulations and references, COM8
Inter-American Development Bank, S17
Inter-American Investment Corporation, S17
Interbank liabilities
    correspondent capital, COM105–07
    correspondent evaluation, COM104–05
    exposure limits and monitoring, COM105
    intraday exposures, COM105
    introduction and purpose, COM104
    laws and regulations references, COM107
    policies and procedures, COM104
    third-party, selection of correspondents by, COM105
Interest on deposits, C118
    advertising, C167
    deposit account requirements, C164–66
    finders' and brokers' fees, C167

Interest on deposits *(continued)*
    introduction and purpose, C164
    laws and regulations references, C167–68
    premiums, C166–67
Interest payment, Truth in Savings Act (TISA), C229
Interest rate adjustments, C9
Interest rate changes (ARM), notice of, C10
Interest rate exposure, COM7
Interest rate-related contracts, COM63, COM66
Interest rate risk, COM66–67, RM15
Interest rates, significantly higher, COM39–40
Interlocks. *See* Management interlocks
Intermediary institutions, C32
    payment order information (travel rule), C34
Internal audit system, COM6
Internal controls
    directors and, T13
    information systems and, COM6
    shareholder services and, T70
Internal Revenue Code (IRC), C166, C185
    charitable trust, T20–21
    collective investment funds (CIFs), T127, T129, T135–36, T137, T138–39
    employee benefit/retirement plans, T32, T34, T35, T38, T42, T43, T44
    trust by agreement, T20
Internal Revenue Service
    Affiliation Schedule (Form 851), C23
    collective investment funds (CIFs), T140–41
    CTR (Form 4789), R14
    Data Center, C20
    employee benefit plans, T37, T38
    FBAR (TD F90-22-1), R16
    international trust services, T74–75
    Model Customer Exemption Statement, C25
Internal transfers, C31
International Bank for Reconstruction and Development, S17
International banking facility (IBF), COM123–24
International banking operations
    accounting for fees on international loans, COM122–23
    allocated transfer risk reserves (ATRR), COM121–22
    changes in, COM110–11, COM117–21 (passim)
    Edge and Agreement corporations. *See* Edge and Agreement corporations
    foreign branches of U.S. banking institutions, COM110–12
    international banking facilities (IBFs), COM123–24
    introduction and purpose, COM110

International banking operations *(continued)*
    laws and regulations references, COM124
    reporting and disclosure third parties, COM122
    supervision and reporting, COM121
International loans, fees on, COM122–23
International Organization Immunities Act of Dec. 29, 1945 (22 U.S.C. 288), C41
International trust services
    foreign trusts, T74–75
    laws/regulations for, T74
    purpose of, T74
    references regarding, T75
Internet banking, RM97–98
Interstate Act (1994), RM9–10
Intraday exposures, COM105
Intraday overdrafts, COM140
"Investable balance" method, C229
Investment Advisors Act (1940), S12, S110, S112
Investment advisory activities, Edge corporation, COM114
Investment advisory agent, T23
Investment area, C15
Investment Company Act (1940), T136, T138–39
    brokerage operations and, S54, S74
    mutual funds and, S110–11, S112, S114, S117
    overview of, S11–12
Investment Company Institute (ICI) v. Camp, T139
Investments, T9
    See also Collective investment funds (CIFs)
Investment test, C51, C55
Investment/treasury activities
    permissible
        debts previously contracted (DPC) stock, S19
        equity investments, S19, S20
        mutual funds, S19–20
        overview of, S16–17
        private placements, S19
        references regarding, S21
        state nonmember banks, S20
        Type III securities, S7, S16, S18
        Type II securities, S7, S16, S17–18
        Type I securities, S7, S16, S17, S18
        Type IV securities, S16, S18
        Type V securities, S16, S18–19
    repurchase agreements
        overview of, S22
        references regarding, S23
        regulatory guidelines, S22–23
        repositioning of, S32–33

Investment/treasury activities *(continued)*
    reverse, S22
    securities dealer selection
        board responsibility in, S34
        minimum considerations in, S34
        overview of, S34
        references regarding, S35
        regulatory guidelines, S34–35
        safekeeping and, S35
    securities lending
        administration of, S25
        Chinese Wall concept, S26
        collateral management, S26–27
        credit analysis, S26
        credit/concentration limits, S26
        employee benefit plans, S28
        FFIEC policy on, S24–25
        finders for, S27–28
        indemnification, S28–29
        overview of, S24
        recordkeeping, S25
        references regarding, S29
        written agreements, S27
    securities transaction reporting
        available-for-sale, S31
        held-to-maturity, S30
        overview of, S30
        references regarding, S31
        trading, S30–31
    unsuitable
        adjusted trading, S33
        corporate/extended settlements, S32
        covered calls, S33
        gains trading, S32
        investment discretionary authority delegation, S33
        "pair offs," S32
        references regarding, S33
        repositioning repurchase agreements, S32–33
        short sales, S33
        "when issued" securities trading, S32
Irrevocable trusts, T28
IRS. *See* Internal Revenue Service

J

Joint accounts, deposit insurance coverage for, C73–74
Joint applicants
    notification of credit, C101
    and signature requirements, C99
Joint credit, and marital status, C96

Joint Notice of Statement Interagency Enforcement Policy for Truth in Lending ("policy guide"), C222
"Joint rule," COM158–59
    exemptions, COM160–61
Joint venture, foreign, COM117, S124–25

K

Keogh Act plans, C74, C165, T32, T35, T44–45, T137, T159
Kickbacks, C177–78
"Know your customer" requirements, C35–36, C37

L

Land. *See* Property
Large customer, definition of, COM25
Laws, Investment Company Act (1940)
    Bank Holding Company Act (BHCA), S8–9, S77, S120–21
    blue sky laws, S13
    for collective investment funds (CIFs), T136–41
    for corporate trusts, T54–55
    for employee benefit/retirement plans, T32–33, T36–44
    environmental, T25–27, T54
    Federal Deposit Insurance Act (FDIA), S9, S20
    Federal Reserve Act, S10, S78, S81, S82, S85, S120, S123
    Glass-Steagall Act
        equity investments and, S19
        overview of, S6
        Section 16, S6–7, S10, S54, S76, S85, S111
        Section 20, S6, S7, S8, S18, S19, S76–84, S114–15, S126
        Section 21, S6, S7–8, S76, S111
        Section 32, S6, S8
        underwriting/dealing and, S6–8, S18, S19, S76–84
    Government Securities Act (GSA) (1986), S99–108
    Home Owners Loan Act (HOLA), S9, S10
        for international trust services, T74
        Investment Advisors Act (1940), S12, S110, S112
    Investment Company Act (1940)
        brokerage operations and, S54, S74
        mutual funds and, S110–11, S112, S114, S117
        overview of, S11–12
    personal trusts for, T24–28
        environmental, T25–27
        federal, T25

Laws, Investment Company Act *(continued)*
    state, T27–28
    Securities Act (1933), S82
    Securities Acts Amendments (1975), S12, S86
    Securities Exchange Act (1934), S10–11, S43, S54, S56, S70, S72, S116
Lease financing
    CEBA Leases, COM127
    federal savings associations requirements, COM128
    finance leases, COM128–29
    full-payout, COM127–28
    general leases, COM129
    general rule, COM126–27
    introduction and purpose, COM126
    laws and regulations references, COM129
    national bank requirements, COM126
    salvage powers, COM129
Leases
    finance, COM187
    real estate appraisals and, COM175
    See also Consumer Leasing Act
Legal risk, RM15, RM18
Lending discrimination, types of, C92–93
Lending examinations, fair, C138–39
Lending limits
    collateral procedures, COM134
    combining loans to separate borrowers, COM134–35
    commitments to advance funds, COM136–39
    definitions, COM132–34
    Edge corporation, COM115–16
    exceptions and exclusions, COM139–40
    general limitations, COM132
    to insiders, COM151
    introduction and purpose, COM132
    laws and regulations references, COM141
    nonconforming loans, COM135–36
    renewals, COM138–39
    savings association exceptions, COM140–41
Lending standards. *See* Real estate lending standards
Lending test, C50–52, C55
Leverage ratio
    minimum, COM69–70
    Tier I, COM51
Liability, disclosure of (CLA), C60–61
Library control
    private library, RM71–72
    production library, RM71
    test library, RM71
Licensing, RM8

Licensing *(continued)*
   dual system of, RM11
   revocations
      conservatorship and, RM186
      foreign banks, RM186–87
      receivership and, RM185–86
Liens, COM175
Lifeline account, C12
Limited purpose institutions, community development test, C52–53
Line grabbing, RM83–84
Liquid funds, Edge corporation, COM114
Liquidity
   rating systems and, RM128, RM133–34
   risk in, RM15, RM18
Liquidity risks
   cash flow/funding, S48
   defined, S45
   management of, S48
   market/product, S48
   monitoring of, S48
Listed corporations, C21–22
Livestock, loans secured by, COM140
Loan application register reporting, C140
Loan/Application Registers, C141, C156–57
Loan balance adjustments, C9
Loan commitment fees, international loans, COM123
Loan contract, under credit practice rules, C66–67
Loan conversions, C171–72
Loan documentation, COM6
   environmental risk program, COM96–97
Loan oversight activities, permissible, secured creditor exemption for UST, COM94–95
Loans, T128–29
   insider. *See* Insiders, loans to
   legally unenforceable, COM140
   margin. *See* Margin loans
   political, COM170
   secured by bank stock, COM145
   special purpose, COM166
   See also Lending limits
Loan to value (LTV), COM181–82
Loan work-out activities, COM95
Loans and extension of credit, definition of, COM132
Logs, RM79–81
"Low balance" method, C229
Low-quality assets, COM12, COM13
LPR, R123

M

Management Consignment exemption, COM161
Management interlocks
   applicability, COM158
   change in circumstances, COM161
   exemptions, COM160–61
   "Interlocks Act," COM158, COM159, COM160
   introduction and purpose, COM158
   laws and regulations references, COM161
   prohibitions, COM158–59
   relationships permitted by statute, COM159–60
"Management official," definition of, COM158
Management report, COM23–24
Managing agent, T23–24
Managing banking institutions, international loans and, COM123
Margin loans
   coverage-purpose loan, COM164
   decline in value of collateral, COM165
   exempted transactions, COM166–67
   introduction and purpose, COM164
   laws and regulations references, COM167
   maximum loan value, COM164
   proposals, COM167
   purpose statement (Form U-1), COM164–65
   single-credit rule, COM165–66
   special purpose loans to brokers/dealers, COM166
   withdrawals/substitutions of cash or collateral, COM166
Margin requirements, affiliate transactions and, COM12–13
Margin stock
   definition of, COM164
   See also Margin loans
Marital status
   and ECOA application processing/evaluation, C96, C98
   request for information of, C94, C139
Market risk, RM15, RM18
Market risk rule, COM67–69
Market risks
   dealers/active position-takers, S46
   defined, S44
   limited end-users, S46–47
   management of, S46–47
Market Valuation Model, COM67
Masquerading, RM83
Maximum loan value, COM164
Means test, COM135
Mellon Order, S115–16

Member bank direct investments, overseas, S123
"Member of the Federal Deposit Insurance Corporation," C77
Metropolitan Statistical Area (MSA), C46, C47, C154, C156, C157
Mini-funds, T129
Minimum Security Devices and Procedures, T85
Minor guardianship, T22
Model Customer Exemption Statement, C25
Modern portfolio theory, T106
Monetary instrument recordkeeping requirements, C30
Monetary Instrument Transaction Records, required information, C27–28
Money laundering, T88
   and filing SAR, COM34–35
Money Laundering and Control Act (MLCA) of 1986, C19
Money Laundering Suppression Act (MLCA) of 1994, C19, C21, C43
Money market deposit account (MMDA), C165–66, COM192
Money orders, C113
Money purchase plans, T34
Monitoring
   environmental risk program, COM97
   interbank liabilities and, COM105
Mortgage funds, T128
Mortgage loans, C197
Mortgage portfolio protection plan (MPPP), C149–50
Mortgages
   high-rate/high fee, C217–19
   nondepository lenders, C154
   reverse, C96, C219–20
   See also Adjustable rate mortgage rules; Truth in Lending Act (TILA)
Mortgage servicing, C179–81
Mortgage-servicing assets (MSAs), COM55
Mortgage servicing rights (MSR), COM54
MSD, R128
MSD-4, R129
MSD-5, R130
MSDW, R131
Multilateral netting, S50
Multinationalism, T74
Multiple creditors or consumers, C195
Municipal bond funds, T128
Municipal securities laws (1975), S12–13
Municipal securities principal, S87
Municipal securities representative, S87
Municipal Securities Rulemaking Board (MSRB), S12

Municipal Securities Rulemaking Board *(continued)*
   Rule G-1, S86–87
   Rule G-2, S87–88
   Rule G-3, S87–88
   Rule G-8, S88–89
   Rule G-8(a)(xi), S93
   Rule G-9, S89
   Rule G-11, S89–90
   Rule G-12, S90–91
   Rule G-13, S91
   Rule G-14, S91
   Rule G-15, S91–92
   Rule G-17, S92
   Rule G-18, S92–93
   Rule G-19, S89, S93–94
   Rule G-20, S94
   Rule G-21, S94
   Rule G-22, S94
   Rule G-23, S94–95
   Rule G-24, S95
   Rule G-25, S95
   Rule G-26, S95
   Rule G-27, S95–96
   Rule G-28, S96
   Rule G-29, S96
   Rule G-30, S96–97
   Rule G-31, S97
   Rule G-32, S97
   Rule G-33, S97
   Rule G-34, S97
   Rule G-35, S97
   Rule G-36, S97–98
   Rule G-37, S89, S98
   Rule G-38, S89, S98
   Rule G-39, S98
Mutual fund holdings, risk weighting, COM60
Mutual funds
   administration of, S114–16
   brokerage operations and, S61–62
   custodianship of, S117
   investment advisers and, S112–13
   investment companies and, S19–20
   Investment Company Act (1940) and, S110–11, S112, S114, S117
   names for, S113–14
   organizing/sponsoring of, S111–12
   overview of, S110–11
   portfolio management, T120–22
      prohibited transaction exemptions, T121–22

Mutual funds *(continued)*
  proprietary, T135
  references regarding, S117
  regulatory examinations and, T158
  reports on, T159
  transfer agent for, T61–62
  transfer agents for, S116–17
Mutual Mortgage Insurance Fund, C161

N

Names on account, ECOA and, C98
NASDAQ, C22–23, T93, T119
  National Market System, COM164
National Association of Securities Dealers (NASD), S11, S56, S63, S68, S69, S70–71
  underwriting/dealing, S78, S99, S106–7
National Automated Clearing House Association (NACHA), RM96
National Bank Act, S54, S112
  Section 12 U.S.C. 24 (Seventh), COM126, COM127–28
  Section 12 U.S.C. 24 (Tenth), COM126
National Bank Surveillance System (NBSS), RM122, RM174–75
National banks, RM6, RM11
National Credit Union Administration (NCUA), RM7
National Credit Union Administration Central Liquidity Facility, COM194
National Flood Insurance Program (NFIP), C144–45, C146, C147
National Flood Insurance Reform Act of 1994, C149
Nationally Recognized Securities Rating Organization (NRSRO), S19
National origin, request for information of, C95
National securities exchange, COM164
"Negative" pledge agreement, COM164
Negotiable order of withdrawal (NOW) account, C112, C166, COM192
Net debit caps, COM76–77, COM78
Net lease basis, COM126
Netting, COM64
Netting contracts
  bilateral, S50
  multilateral, S50
Network protection, RM76–77
New accounts, C114, C227–28
New York Stock Exchange, C22–23, T66, T96, T128
Night depository, C120

"No cost" loans, C173
Nominee registration, T84
Nonbank financial institution (NBFI), C31
Nonconforming loans, COM135–36
Nondeposit investment products, S57
Nondepository institutions, RM7
  registration of, C43
Nondepository mortgage lenders, C154
Nonpersonal time deposits, COM193
Nonsegregated disclosures, C60
"No point" loans, C173
Note issuance facilities (NIFs), COM62
Notice 96-65, T75
Notice 97-42, T75
Notice of error, C89
NOW account. *See* Negotiable order of withdrawal (NOW) account

O

OAEM rated assets, COM13
Obligations, T128–29
OECD countries, 58n1, definition of
  banks in, balance sheet assets, COM58, COM59
Office of Foreign Assets Control (OFAC), COM100–102, T88
Office of the Comptroller of the Currency (OCC)
  brokerage operations, S55, S61, S64, S66, S70
  capital adequacy, COM52
  CC 7029-06a, R63
  CC 7029-06b, R64
  CC 7029-07, R63
  CC 7610-02, R66
  director responsibility and, T8
  environmental compliance and, T26–27
  Glass-Steagall Act and, S7
  Interlocks Act, COM158
  investment activities, S16, S17, S19, S20
  lease financing, COM126, COM127
  mutual funds and, S111, S112, S113–16
  nonconforming loans, COM135–36
  overseas activities, S120
  portfolio management and
    affiliated brokerage, T111–12
    derivatives, T115–16
    mutual funds, T120–21
    option investments, T124
  rating systems and, RM125, RM146, RM175
  real estate lending standards, COM180
  real estate ownership, COM186–90 (passim)

32 Compliance Link

Office of the Comptroller of the Currency *(continued)*
   regulatory enforcement and, RM185–87
   regulatory examination and, RM48, T158
   regulatory system and, RM11
   risk-focused examination and, RM14–15, RM16
   underwriting/dealing, S84, S99, S101–2
Office of Thrift Supervision (OTS), T86–87
   capital adequacy, COM52
   dividend regulations, COM84–86
   independent audits, COM22
   Interlocks Act, COM158
   lease financing, COM126, COM128
   loans to insiders, COM154
   Market Valuation Model, COM67
   OTS 1313 (TFR), R33–35
   proposed interest rate risk (IRR), COM66–67
   rating systems and, RM125–26
   real estate lending standards, COM180
   regulatory examination and, RM48
   risk-focused examination and, RM17–18
   Thrift Bulletin, COM67
Officer of Federal Contract Compliance Programs, C109, C118
"On us" checks, C113–14, C118
$100 rule, C113
Open-end credit, C200
   advertising credit terms, C208
   billing error resolution, C207–08
   cardholder claims and defenses, C207
   cardholder liability, C206
   crediting payments and refunds, C205–06
   definition of, C193
   disclosures. *See* Open-end credit disclosures
   home equity lines of credit (HELCs), C209–12
   issuance of credit cards, C201
   prohibition offsets, C206
   transaction identification, C204–05
Open-end credit disclosures
   additional, C204
   annual percentage rate (APR), C196
   application, C201–2
   finance charge, C197
   home equity lines of credit (HELCs), C209–10
   initial statement, C202–3
   periodic statement, C203–4
   required, C200
   subsequent, C203
   variable rate information, C203, C210
Open-end investment company. *See* Mutual funds

Operational risk, RM15, RM17
Operation risks
   defined, S45
   documentation, S49
   duty separation, S49
   management of, S49
   personnel quality, S49
   systems quality, S49
   valuation issues, S49
Operations. *See* Trust department operations
Opting-out, RM9–10
Options
   call, S38
   put, S38
Options Clearing Corporation, T124
Options investments, T124
Originated mortgage servicing rights (OMSR), COM55
Originator, in funds transfers, C31
Originator's institution
   in funds transfers, C31–33
   payment orders information (travel rule), C33–34
OTC. *See* Over-the-counter (OTC)
Other real estate owned (OREO). *See* Real estate ownership, other real estate owned (OREO)
OTS 1313 (TFR), R33–35
Outsourcing
   information systems, RM60
   internal audits, RM30–31
Overdrafts
   daylight
      administration of, COM79
      cap multiples, COM78
      covered institutions, COM76
      de minimis cap, COM76, COM78–79
      foreign banks, COM80
      introduction and purpose, COM76
      net debit caps, COM76–77, COM78
      pricing, COM79–80
      references, COM80
      self-assessment cap, COM77–78
      zero cap, COM79
   intraday, COM140
   loans to insiders, COM150–51
   repeated, C115
Overseas activities
   debt-for-equity conversions
      FRB approval of, S129
      ownership restrictions, S128–29
   foreign branches

Overseas activities *(continued)*
    branch subsidiaries, S122
    investments, S122
    repurchase agreements, S123
    underwriting, S121–22
    investments
        foreign branches, S122
        FRB approval of, S124
        member bank direct, S123
        U.S. activities, S123–24
    joint ventures, S124–25
    operating structures for, S121
    overseas subsidiaries, S125–28
        investments, S126
        underwriting, S126–27
    overview of, S120
    portfolio investments, S124–25
    references regarding, S129
    statutes/regulations for
        Bank Holding Company Act (BHCA), S120–21
        Federal Reserve Act, S120, S123
        Regulation K, S121, S124, S126, S127–28
Overt discrimination, C92
Over-the-counter (OTC)
    derivatives, COM68, COM69
    stocks, COM164

P

Paid Outside of Closing (P.O.C.), C173
"Pair offs," S32
Partnerships, loans to, COM135
Partnership Tax Return, T140
Party-in-interest, T40–42, T112, T140
Passbook savings accounts, C164
Pass-through accounts, C28–29
Pass-through insurance, C74–76
Payable through accounts (PTA), C28–29
Paying agent, T51
Payment and loan balance adjustments, C9
Payment changes (ARM), notice of, C10
Payment order information (travel rule), C33–35
Payment orders, C31–33
Payment plans, credit practice rules and, C67
Payments, insurance, C60
Payments and collections, Edge corporation, COM114
Payment system risks, COM76
Payroll deduction, credit practice rules and, C67
Payroll withdrawals, CTR reporting and, C25
PD 1025, R51

Penalties
    civil money
        in general, RM182–83
        for holding companies, RM183–84
        reports and, RM183
        sentencing guidelines and, RM191
Penalties, disclosure of (CLA), C60
Pension Benefit Guarantee Corporation (PBGC), T33–34, T37, T38
Pension plans. *See* Employee benefit/retirement plans
Performance evaluations, CRA, C46, C48, C49–50
Periodic statement disclosures
    Truth in Lending Act (TILA), C203–4
    Truth in Savings Act (TISA), C229
Periodic statement disclosures, C82–83
Perpetual preferred stock, COM52
Person, definition of, COM132
Personal identification number (PIN), C201, RM95, RM98–100
Personal trusts
    administration of, T24
    agency accounts, T22–24
        attorney-in-fact, T24
        custodianship, T23
        escrow agent, T23
        investment advisory agent, T23
        managing agent, T23–24
        safekeeping, T24
    charitable, T20–21
    co-fiduciary, T22
    court-ordered, T21
    estate settlement, T18–19
    FDIC insurance for, T28
    guardianship, T22
    irrevocable, T28
    laws/regulations for, T24–28
        environmental, T25–27
        federal, T25
        state, T27–28
    references regarding, T28–29
    revocable, T28
    trust by agreement, T19–20
    trust by declaration, T19–20
    trust under will, T19
Personnel
    brokerage operations
        policies/procedures, S69
        qualifications/training, S63
        registration, S69–70

Personnel *(continued)*
    transactions, S73–74
    compliance function and, RM42–43
    derivatives, S49
    development of, T10–11
    ethics for, T11
    fingerprinting of, T67
    information systems and
        application programmers, RM64–65
        system programmers, RM65
    regulatory examination and, RM51
    underwriting/dealing, S87–88
    See also Directors
Physical commodity transactions, S50–51
Piggyback arrangement, T86, T96
Piggybacking, RM83
PINs. *See* Personal identification number
Pledge requirements, T82
Point-of-sale (POS) transaction, RM94–95
Point system, C95
Policies, environmental risk program, COM96
Policies/procedures
    brokerage placement practices, T9–10
    conflict of interest, T10
    inside information, T10
    investments, T9
    for personnel, T10–12
    service pricing, T11–12
Policy Statement on Discrimination in Lending, C138
Political action committee (PAC), COM170–71
Political contributions, COM170–71
Political loans, COM170
Political subdivision general obligations, COM140
Pooled funds, T126
Portfolio investments, foreign, COM116, COM117, S124–25
Portfolio management
    beneficiary needs
        account termination, T113
        human dimension, T113
        income, T112
        principal distributions, T112
        purchasing power, T113
        tax-exemptions, T112–13
    conflict of interest in
        affiliated brokerage, T111–12
        Chinese Wall concept, T110
        conflict transactions, T106–7
        financial benefits, T110–11

Portfolio management *(continued)*
    inside information, T110–11
    own-bank/affiliate securities, T108
    related parties/organizations, T109–10
    forward contracts, T123–24
    investment authority, T104–5
    mutual funds, T120–22
        prohibited transaction exemptions, T121–22
    options investments, T124
    prudent person rule, T105–6
        modern portfolio theory, T106
    purpose of, T104
    references regarding, T124
    repurchase agreements, T123
    restricted securities, T118–20
        qualified institutional buyers (QIBs), T119–20
    risk management, T113–17
        derivatives, T115–17
        high risk assets, T117
        securities documentation/review, T117–18
    syndications, T111
Postal Service, money orders, C113
Postdated checks, C116
    prohibited practices involving, C133
Postforeclosure activities, secured creditor exemption and, COM91–92
Poverty levels, and distressed community, C14
Power limitations, RM8
Preapproval credit programs, C101, COM150
Preauthorized transfer disclosures, C83–84
Preferred stock, perpetual, COM52
Preforeclosure activities, secured creditor exemption and, COM90–91
Prelending activities, permissible, secured creditor exemption for UST, COM94
Premiums on demand deposit accounts, C166–67
Prequalification credit programs, C101
Prescreening, C93, C126–27
    nondiscrimination in, C137
Presettlement credit risk, S47
Price risk, RM15
PricewaterhouseCoopers Regulatory Advisory Service, C5, COM3
Price WaterhouseCoopers Trust Regulatory Handbook for Financial Institutions, The, C76
Pricing policy (for services), T11–12
Principal/income separation, T80
Principal shareholders
    definition of, COM149

Principal shareholders *(continued)*
    filing of FFIEC 004, COM154
Privacy. *See* Right to Financial Privacy Act (RFPA)
Private library, RM71–72
Private placements, S19
Production library, RM71
Products, S55, S57, S58, S61, S80, S113–14
Profit-sharing plans, T34
Prohibited Transaction Exemption (PTE) 81–6, S28
Prohibited Transaction Exemption (PTE) 82–63, S28
Prohibition, COM144
Prompt corrective action (PCA)
    capital categories, C75, C76, COM38–39, COM49, COM70–72, COM77
    determining a bank or thrift capital category, COM72–73
    introduction, COM70
Property, seizure of, C37
Property loans, C171
Protection Act (1996), T25–26
Proxy voting, T12
Prudential restrictions, on Edge corporations, COM115–16
"Prudential standards," COM104–5
Prudent person rule
    common law, T105–6
    federal, T105–6
    modern portfolio theory, T106
    prudent investor rule, T106
PTE 75-1, T122
PTE 77-3, T122
PTE 77-4, T44, T121, T122
PTE 81-6, T43
PTE 84-24, T122
Public disclosure, COM153
Purchased credit card relationship (PCCR), COM54, COM55
Purchase option, disclosure of (CLA), C60
Purpose loans/credit, COM164, COM165–66
Purpose test, COM135
Pyramiding, C68

Q

Qualified institutional buyers (QIBs), T119–20
Qualified report, RM34–35
Qualifying activities as specified by BEA, C13, C14, C15
"Quality of assistance," C92
Quarterly Report of Selected Deposits, Vault Cash and Reservable Liabilities (Form FR 2910q), COM194
Quotations, S91

R

Race, request for information of, C95, C139
Railroad Retirement Board, C185
Ratings systems
    BOPEC
        bank condition, RM156–57
        capital adequacy, RM162–65
        consolidated earnings, RM160–62
        finances, RM154
        management, RM154–56
        nonbank condition, RM157–59
        overview of, RM122, RM151–54
        parent company, RM159–60
        risk management, RM165–67
    Community Reinvestment performance, RM122
    Consumer Compliance
        composite ratings, RM168–70
        FDIC and, RM170
        overview of, RM122, RM167–68
    five-point scale for, RM122–25
    foreign banks
        annual examination plan, RM150–51
        Combined rating, RM148
        ROCA, RM122, RM146–48, RM150
        SOSA, RM122, RM149–50
    off-site
        NBSS, RM122, RM174–75
        SEER, RM122, RM174–75
    Uniform Financial Institutions Rating System (UFIRS) (CAMELS), RM122, RM125–37
        asset quality, RM128, RM129–30
        CAMELS acronym, RM128
        capital adequacy, RM128, RM129
        earnings, RM128, RM132–33
        FDICIA connection, RM136–37
        liquidity, RM128, RM133–34
        management/administration, RM128, RM130–32
        market risk sensitivity, RM128, RM134–36
        overview of, RM125–27
        performance evaluation, RM128–36
    Uniform Interagency/Data Processing Organizations, RM122, RM170–74
        audits, RM171
        computer operations, RM174
        management, RM172–73
        systems/programming, RM173
    Uniform Interagency Trust Rating System (UITRS), RM122, RM137–46

Ratings systems *(continued)*
    account administration, RM141–42
    asset administration, RM140–41
    conflict of interest, RM142–43
    earnings/volume trends/prospects, RM143–45
    operations/controls/audits, RM139–40
    proposed changes for, RM145–46
    supervision/organization, RM138–39
Readily marketable collateral, COM133–34
Real estate. *See* Fair Housing Act; Real Estate Settlement Procedures Act (RESPA)
Real estate appraisals
    appraiser independence, COM177–78
    certification/licensing requirements, COM177
    introduction and purpose, COM174
    laws and regulations references, COM178
    nonappraisal evaluations, COM176
    OREO, COM190
    standards for, COM177
    transactions covered, COM174
    transactions requiring, COM174–77
Real estate investment funds, T128, T134
Real estate lending standards
    exceptions and exclusions, COM182–83
    guidelines applicability, COM180
    introduction and purpose, COM180
    laws and regulations references, COM183
    policy formation, COM180–81
    supervisory LTV limits, COM181–82
    supervisory review, COM183
Real estate notes, COM175
Real estate ownership
    bank premises, COM186–87
    finance leases, COM187
    future expansion, COM187
    general limitation, COM186
    introduction and purpose, COM186
    law and regulation references, COM190
    other real estate owned (OREO), COM187, COM188
        accounting requirements, COM190
        appraisals, COM189–90
        disposal of, COM188–89
        holding period, COM189
        improvements to, COM189–90
Real estate related financial transaction, COM174
Real Estate Settlement Procedures Act (RESPA)
    affiliated business arrangements, C178–79
    dealer loans, C172
    disclosures, C179–82

Real Estate Settlement Procedures Act *(continued)*
    escrow accounts, C175–76
    escrow statements, C176–77
    fees for required statements, C179
    FHA loan prepayment disclosures, C182
    good faith estimate of settlement costs, C173–74
    identity of person receiving benefit, C179
    introduction and purpose, C171
    laws and regulations references, C182
    mortgage servicing, C179–81
    referral fees and kickbacks, C177–78
    special information booklet, C172–73
    title companies, C179
    transactions covered and not covered, C171–72
    Uniform Settlement Statement (HUD-1 and HUD-1A), C174–75
Realized value, C60–61
Receipts, from electronic terminals, C82
Recordkeeping
    brokerage operations, S66–67
    directors and, T12
    securities lending, S25
    shareholder services and, T69
    turnaround performance requirements, T66
    underwriting/dealing, S88–89, S101–2
Records
    compliance function and
        establishment of, RM43
        review of, RM43–44
    regulatory examination and, RM51
"Recourse" rule revision, COM50–51
Redeposited checks, C115
Reference credit, S40
Referral fees, C177–78
Refinancing, C194–95
    real estate appraisals and, COM175
Registrar, T60-61
Registration
    brokerage personnel, S69–70
    broker-dealer, S56, S99–100
    Regulation 9, T74, T120, T129, T130–31, T132, T133, T136, T139, T140
    Regulation 9.4, T8
    Regulation 9.10(a), T81
    Regulation 9.12, T120
    Regulation 9(a)(1), T126
    Regulation 9(a)(2), T126
    Regulation B, C91, C95, C100, C101, C103, C104, C125

Registration *(continued)*
 Regulation C, C154, C156
 Regulation CC, C112, C114, C116, C118, C121, C229
 Regulation D, COM192–93 (passim)
 Regulation DD, C167, C224–25
 Regulation DD, 167
  disclosures, C227–29, C231
  interim rule amending, C226–27
 Regulation E, C80, C86
 Regulation F, COM104–7
 Regulation K, COM110–24, COM119, COM122, S9, S121, S124, S126, S127–28, T74
 Regulation O, COM112, COM148, COM149, COM154
 Regulation Q, C164
 Regulation R, S8
 Regulation S, C187
 Regulation T, C85, T94
 Regulation U
  exemptions, COM165–66
  proposed changes, COM166
 Regulation U, COM164–65, T93–94
 Regulation X, C171, T94
 Regulation Y, COM117, COM118, COM119, S8–9, S54–55, S79, S113, S114
 Regulation Z, C86, C191, C192–94, C196, C197, C217–20
 Regulation Z, 86, 191, 192–94, 196, 197
 See also Truth in Lending Act (TILA)
Regulatory Advisory Services, PricewaterhouseCoopers, C5, COM3
Regulatory consumer compliance examination, C4–5
Regulatory enforcement
 formal, RM178–84
  cease-and-desist orders, RM179–80
  cease-and-desist orders, temporary, RM180
  civil money penalty, RM182–83
  civil money penalty holding companies, RM183–84
  civil money penalty reports, RM183
  institution-affiliated party removal, RM180–82
  insurance termination, RM184
 informal, RM178
 license revocations
  conservatorship, RM186
  foreign bank office termination, RM186–87
  receivership, RM185–86
 overview of, RM178
Regulatory examination
 management of
  documentation, RM50
  examination coordinator, RM50–51

Regulatory examination *(continued)*
  examiner treatment, RM52
  First Day Letter, RM49
  information control, RM51
  personnel training, RM51
  policy awareness, RM52
  prior exception corrections, RM52
 objectives of, RM48–49
 procedures for, RM49
 process of, RM48
 records for, RM51
 reports for, RM48–49
 See also Risk-focused examination
Regulatory examinations
 annual regulatory reports, T158–60
 mutual funds, T158
 new developments in, T157–58
 performance ratings, T156
 purpose of, T154
 references regarding, T160
 risk management, T154–58
  risk analysis phase, T154–55
  transaction testing phase, T155–56
Regulatory Reporting Handbook, The, COM35
Regulatory Standards exemption, COM160
Regulatory system
 bank holding companies, RM9
  geographic restrictions, RM10
  securities activities, RM10–11
 commercial banks, RM6
  geographic restrictions, RM9–10
 credit unions, RM7
 deposit insurance, RM6, RM7, RM8, RM11–12
 federal/state regulations, RM11–12
  dual system of, RM11
 geographic restrictions
  bank holding companies, RM10
  commercial banks, RM9–10
  de novo branches, RM10
  Interstate Act (1994), RM9–10
  opting-out, RM9–10
  savings associations, RM10
 licensing/approval, RM8
 national banks, RM6, RM11
 nondepository institutions, RM7
 power limitations, RM8
 reserve requirements, RM8–9
 savings associations, RM7
  geographic restrictions, RM10

Regulatory system *(continued)*
    savings and loan holding company, RM9
    unitary savings and loan holding company, RM9
  securities activities, RM10–11
  state banks, RM6, RM11
  supervisory oversight, RM8
Rehabilitation Act of 1973, C109
Related interests, COM153, COM154–55
  definition of, COM149
Relevant Metropolitan Statistical Area (RMSA), COM159
Religion, request for information of, C95
Renewals, real estate appraisals and, COM175
Renewed deposits, C75
Report FFIEC 004, COM154
Report of Certain Eurocurrency Transactions (FR 2950/2951), COM195
Report of Condition and Income, COM12, COM151
Report of Condition and Income (Call Report), RM183
Report of Foreign Bank and Financial Account Form TDF 90-22.1, C39
Report of International Transportation of Currency or Monetary Instrument, Form 4790, C37
Report of Selected Deposits, Vault Cash and Reservable Liabilities, Quarterly (Form FR 2910q), COM194
Report of Supervisory Activities (ROSA), T156
Report of Total Deposits and Reservable Liabilities, Annual, (Form FR 2910a), COM195
Report of Transaction Accounts, Other Deposits and Vault Cash (Form FR2900), COM194
Reporting
  available-for-sale securities, S31
  FOCUS reports, S81
  FR Y-20 reports, S81
  held-to-maturity securities, S30
  overview of, S30
  references regarding, S31
  securities trading, S30–31
  underwriting/dealing, S91
Reports
  annual, T70, T158–60
  Annual Report of Trust Assets, T158–60
  on audits, T151
  on collective investment funds (CIFs), T131–32, T159
  on corporate trusts, T159
  Currency or Monetary Instruments Report (CMIR), T87–88
  Currency Transaction Report (CTR), T87
  external audits
    adverse, RM35

Reports *(continued)*
    disclaimer, RM35
    qualified, RM34–35
    standards for, RM33
    unqualified, RM34
  information systems, RM59
  internal audits, RM29
  quarterly, T92–93
  regulatory examination, RM48–49
  Report of Supervisory Activities (ROSA), T156
Repurchase agreements, T123
  overseas activities and, S123
  overview of, S22
  references regarding, S23
  regulatory guidelines, S22–23
  repositioning of, S32–33
  reverse, S22
  underwriting/dealing
    blind pooled, S106
    hold-in-custody, S23, S104–6
Reputation risk, RM15
Requests for disclosures, C228
Rescission, consumer right to, C220–22
Reserve requirements, RM8–9
Reserves on deposits
  1998 changes to, COM195
  affected institutions, COM192
  computation of, COM195
  definitions, COM192–93
  introduction and purpose, COM192
  laws and regulations references, COM196
  maintenance of reserves, COM193–94
  reporting requirements, COM194–95
  reserve requirements, COM192, COM193
Residential loans, C136
Residential-related securities, C136
Residual value, C60–61
Resolution Trust Corporation (RTC), balance sheet assets, COM58, COM59
Resource Conservation and Recovery Act of 1986, COM88, T25–26
Restatement of the Law of Trusts, The, T25
Restatement (Third) of the Law of Trusts, The, T106
Restricted lists, S73
Restricted securities, T118–20
  qualified institutional buyers (QIBs), T119–20
Restructured international loans, COM122
Retail businesses, CTR reporting and, C25
Retirement accounts, deposit insurance coverage for, C74

Retirement plans. *See* Employee benefit/retirement plans
Reverse mortgage transactions, C96, C219–20
Review, environmental, COM96
Revocable trusts, T28
Revolving underwriting facilities (RUFs), COM62
Riegle-Neal Interstate Banking and Branching Efficiency Act (1994), RM9–10
Right of rescission, C220–22
Right to Financial Privacy Act (RFPA), C30
    agency certification, C184
    bank compliance, C186
    civil liability, C187
    customer notice, C184
    customer notice prohibited, C188
    customer protection, C184
    exceptions to certificate of compliance, C185
    form of request, C185–86
    introduction and purpose, C184
    laws and regulations references, C188
    record-keeping requirements, C186–87
    reimbursement and exceptions, C187
Right to Privacy Act, safe harbor of, COM35
Risk-based capital. *See* Capital adequacy, risk-based standards
Risk-focused examination
    agency differences in, RM14–15
        risk categories, RM15
    audits and, RM20
    compliance risk, RM15, RM18–19
    credit risk, RM15, RM17, RM19, RM20
    FDIC and, RM16–17
    Federal Reserve System and, RM14–15
    foreign exchange risk, RM15
    FRB and, RM16
    interest rate risk, RM15
    legal risk, RM15, RM18
    liquidity risk, RM15, RM18
    market risk, RM15, RM18
    OCC and, RM14–15, RM16
    operational risk, RM15, RM17
    OTS and, RM17–18
    price risk, RM15
    process of, RM16
    renewed emphasis on, RM14
    reputation risk, RM15
    risk management in, RM19–20
    strategic risk, RM15, RM18
    transaction risk, RM15
Riskless principal transactions, S55, S93
Risk management
    counterparty credit risk, S47–48
        credit authorization, S47
        defined, S44
        monitoring of, S48
        presettlement, S47
        settlement, S47
    directors and, T13
    legal risks, S49–51
        bilateral netting, S50
        multilateral netting, S50
        physical commodity transactions, S50–51
    liquidity risks, S48
        cash flow/funding, S48
        defined, S45
        market/product, S48
        monitoring of, S48
    market risks, S46–47
        dealers/active position-takers, S46
        defined, S44
        limited end-users, S46–47
    operation risks, S49
        defined, S45
        documentation, S49
        duty separation, S49
        personnel quality, S49
        systems quality, S49
        valuation issues, S49
    in portfolio management, T113–17
        derivatives, T115–17
        high risk assets, T117
    regulatory examinations and, T154–58
    senior management supervision
        audit coverage, S46
        risk responsibility, S45–46
        risk systems, S46
        written policies/procedures, S45
    in trust operations, T88
Risk management reports, COM7
Risk-weighted assets. *See* Capital adequacy, risk-weighted assets
ROCA rating system, RM122, RM146–48, RM150
Rollovers, C74
Rule 10b-5, S72, T10
Rule 15c2-12, S97–98
Rule 17A, T50
Rule 17Ad-2, T63, T64, T66
Rule 17Ad-4(b), T68, T70
Rule 17Ad-5, T65

Rule 17Ad-6, T63
Rule 17Ad-7, T66
Rule 17Ad-10, T60
Rule 17Ad-10(g), T69
Rule 17Ad-11(b)(1), T69
Rule 17Ad-11(c), T69
Rule 17Ad-11(d)(1), T69
Rule 17Ad-11(d)(2), T69
Rule 17Ad-13(a), T70
Rule 17Ad-15, T59
Rule 17Ad-22, T70
Rule 17f-2, T67
Rule 17j-1, S74
Rule 81-100, T133, T140
Rule 101, T148–49
Rule 144, T63–64, T118–19
Rule 144A, S19, T119–20
Rule 180, T137
Rule 387, T96
Rule 496, T66
Rule 891, T66
Rules
   See also Municipal Securities Rulemaking Board (MSRB)

S

Safe Harbor, COM35, S43
   limited, C23
   restricted securities and, T119
   soft dollars and, T94–95
Safekeeping
   dual control, T85
   duty separation, T85
   limited trust access, T85
   off-premise custody, T86
   on-premise custody, T84–85
   in personal trusts, T24
   piggyback arrangement, T86, T96
   securities dealer selection, S35
   shareholder services and, T70
   underwriting/dealing, S102–4
   U.S. government securities, T86–87
   vault protection, T85
Safekeeping agreement, COM164
Sallie Mae, COM140
Salvage powers, leasing, COM129
Sanctions. *See* Foreign asset controls
SAR, R44–48
Savings accounts, COM192

Savings and Loan Holding Company Act, RM184
Savings Association Insurance Fund (SAIF), C72, RM7
Savings associations, RM7
   affiliate transactions restrictions for, COM15–16
   balance sheet assets, COM58
   dividends and, COM84–86
   FIRREA restrictions, COM82
   geographic restrictions, RM10
   insider loans and, COM153–55
   leasing requirements for Federal, COM128
   lending limit exceptions, COM140–41
   minimum leverage ratio requirements, COM69–70
   official sign for, C77
   OTS requirements for, COM67, COM82, COM84–86
   and risk-weighted mutual funds, COM60
   savings and loan holding company, RM9
   and Tier I capital, COM52
   unitary savings and loan holding company, RM9
Savings (passbook) account, C164
Schedule A, T159
Schedule B, T159
Schedule C, T159
Schedule D, T159
Schedule E, T160
Schedule RC-M, COM190
Secondary market transactions, C172
Secondary mortgage market, C136
Secretary of Housing and Urban Development, C103
Section 3(a), T138
Section 3(a)(2), T137
Section 3(a)(11), T137
Section 3(a)(38), T119
Section 3(c)(3), T138
Section 3(c)(11), T138
Section 4(1), T118
Section 4(4), T119
Section 4(c)(8), S8, S77
Section 4(c)(13), S9, S120
Section 9.18, T129, T130, T139
Section 9.18(a)(1), T127, T129, T133, T140
Section 9.18(a)(2), T127, T129, T134, T140
Section 9.18(b), T129
Section 9.18(b)(1), T130
Section 9.18(ii)(B), T133
Section 10(b), T10
Section 10b, S72
Section 12, T50, T62
Section 12.3, T89
Section 12.4, T91

Section 12 U.S.C. 24 (Seventh), COM126, COM127–28
Section 12 U.S.C. 24 (Tenth), COM126
Section 12 U.S.C. 84, COM132, COM136, COM139
Section 16, S6-7, S10, S54, S76, S85, S111
Section 17A, S116
Section 20, S6, S7, S8, S18, S19, S76–84, S114–15, S126
Section 21, S6, S7-8, S76, S111, T139
Section 22(g), COM148
Section 22(h), COM148
Section 23A, S10, S78, S82, S84, S85
Section 23B, S10, S78, S81, S82, S84, S85
Section 23B(c), S82
Section 24, S54
Section 25, S120
Section 25(a), COM113
Section 28(e), T94–95
Section 32, S6, S8
Section 36, COM22
Section 56, COM60, COM82
Section 72(p), T42
Section 121, COM26
Section 304, T54
Section 310, T54
Section 368(a)(2)(ii), T136
Section 401, T137, T138
Section 401(a), T44, T129
Section 401C, T38
Section 401(c)(1), T137
Section 402C, T38
Section 403(b), T43
Section 404, T38, T44, T137
Section 404(a)(1), T96
Section 405, T39–40
Section 406(a), T43, T122
Section 406(b), T112, T122
Section 406(b)(3), T122
Section 406C, T40
Section 407, T36, T40–41
Section 408, T35, T137, T138, T140
Section 408(b)(4), T36–37
Section 408C, T41
Section 416, T43
Section 501, T140
Section 501(a), T20, T129
Section 501(c)(3), T20, T21
Section 509, T21
Section 584, T129, T140
Section 2550.404(b)(1), T134
Section 4975, T43

Section 6032, T140
Section II(c), T122
Section III(b), T122
Section III(f), T122
Section T406, 40, T38, T43, T140
Section T407(a), 40, T38, T43
Secured creditor exemption, COM89, COM90–92
    for underground storage tanks (USTs), COM90, COM93–95
Secured loans, COM132, COM139
Securities Act (1933), S6, S10, S11, S43, S82, T54, T118–19, T137–38
    Amendments (1975), S12, S86
Securities activities, RM10–11
Securities and Exchange Commission, C23, C193
Securities dealer selection
    overview of, S34
    references regarding, S35
    regulatory guidelines for
        board responsibility, S34
        minimum considerations, S34
        safekeeping, S35
Securities documentation/review, T117–18
Securities exchange, COM164
Securities Exchange Act (1934), S10–11, S43, S54, S56, S70, S72, S116
    corporate trusts, T50
    employee/benefit retirement plans, T43–44
    inside information, T10
    safe harbor, T94–95
    shareholder services, T62
Securities Exchange Commission (SEC)
    annual reports and, T70
    brokerage operations, S56, S61–62, S72–73, S74
    derivatives and, S41–44
    fingerprinting requirements, T67
    Government Securities Act (GSA) and, S10
    Institutional Delivery System, T96
    internal controls evaluation, T70
    Investment Company Act (1940) and, S11–12, S110, S112, S114
    lost/stolen securities, T66–67
    mutual funds and, S110, S111, S112, S113–14, S115, S116
    private placements, S19
    recordkeeping and, T68–69
    restricted securities, T118–20
    Securities Act (1933) and, S10
    Securities Acts Amendments (1975) and, S12, S86
    Securities Exchange Act (1934) and, S10–11, S116

42 Compliance Link

Securities Exchange Commission (SEC) *(continued)*
   transfer agents and, T59, T60, T62
   turnaround performance requirements, T63–66
   underwriting/dealing, S78, S82, S86, S97–98, S100, S101
Securities income processing, T82–83
Securities Information Center (SIC), T66
Securities Investor Protection Corporation, S60
Securities lending, T96–99
   administration of, S25
   borrower credit analysis, T97
   cash collateral, T98
   collateral, S26–29, T98–99
      management of, S26–27
   collateral margins, T97–98
   credit
      analysis of, S26
      limits of, S26
   employee benefit plans, S28
   FFIEC policy on, S24–25
   finders for, S27–28
   indemnification, S28–29
   lending agreement, T97
   letters of credit, T99
   overview of, S24
   recordkeeping, S25
   references regarding, S29
   written agreements, S27
Securities self-regulatory organizations (SSROs), S70
Securities trade processing, T88–91
   best execution, T89, T94
   quarterly reports, T92–93
   trade confirmation, T91–92
   trade execution, T90–91
   trade orders, T89–90
   trade policies/procedures, T92
Securities trading
   adjusted, S33
   gains trading, S32
   reporting of, S30–31
   trading vs. dealing, S77
   "when issued," S205
Securities Transfer Agents Medallion Program (STAMP), T59
Security
   devices, COM32–33
   See also Foreign asset controls
Security interest
   charges, C216
   credit practice rules and, C66, C67

Security interest *(continued)*
   disclosure of (CLA), C60
   information, C215
Security officer, COM32, COM33
Security program, COM32, COM33
Segregated deposit accounts, loans secured by, COM139
Seizure of property, C37
Self-administered bank employee trusts, T36–37
Self-assessment cap, COM77–78
Self-employed retirement trusts, T35
"Senior executive officer," definition of, COM18
Sentencing guidelines
   compliance program and
      effective elements of, RM190–91
      importance of, RM190
   internal reporting systems, RM192
   penalty range, RM191
   purpose of, RM190
   voluntary disclosure and, RM191–92
Separate accounts, ECOA and, C98
"Separately identifiable bank department," S86–87
Separate maintenance income, request for information of, C94
SEPs, T32
Service bureaus, business recovery planning and, COM45
Service test, C51–52, C55
Servicing, mortgage, C179–81
Settlement costs, good faith estimate of, C173–74
Settlement Costs and You, C172
Settlements
   corporate/extended, S32
   risks in, S45, S47
   underwriting/dealing, S90–91
Sex, request for information of, C94, C139
Share draft accounts, COM192
Shareholder Communications Act (1985), T99
Shareholder services
   annual reports, T70
   covered securities, T62
   exchange agent, T70
   fingerprinting requirements, T67
   funds/securities safekeeping, T70
   internal controls evaluation, T70
   lost/stolen securities program, T66–67
   recordkeeping, T69
      turnaround performance requirements, T66
   references regarding, T70–71
   registrar functions, T60–61
   securityholder file, T68–69

Shareholder services *(continued)*
   transfer agent, T58–60
      for mutual funds, T61–62
      registration of, T62
      turnaround performance requirements, T63–66
         business expansion limitations, T64
         exemptions, T65
         recordkeeping, T66
         written inquiry turnaround, T65
Short sales, S33
Short-term investment fund (STIF), T128, T133
Signature requirements, ECOA and, C98–99
Significantly higher interest rates, definition of, COM39–40
Significantly undercapitalized institutions, COM49, COM72
Signs, required, C76–77
   "Equal Housing Lender" logo & poster, C137, C139
   Truth in Savings Act (TISA), C231
Single-credit rule, COM165–66
Single ownership accounts, deposit insurance coverage for, C73
Small Business Job Protection Act (1996), T74–75, T135
Small business loans, C55
Small farm loans, C55
Small-institution performance standards, C50, C53, C55
Smart cards, RM95
Social Security Administration, C185
Soft dollars
   directed brokerage, T95–96
   safe harbor, T94–95
   third-party research, T95
Software
   backup for, RM87–88
   implementation of, RM63
   selection of, RM62
   See also Computer software & systems
SOSA rating system, RM122, RM149–50
Special Flood Hazard Areas (SFHA), C144, C145, C146, C147–48
"Specially Designated Nationals and Blocked Entities," COM101
Specially Designated Nationals and Blocked Persons, COM101
"Specially Designated Nationals" (SDNs), COM101
"Specially Designated Terrorists" (SDTs), COM101
Special purpose loans, COM166
Specifically enumerated businesses, CTR reporting and, C25
Spendthrift guardianship, T22

Spouses
   and ECOA application processing/evaluation, C96–97
   request for information of, C93–94
   signature requirements, C99
SSF 1604, R52
Staff appraisers, COM177
Stale dated checks, C115
Standard Flood Hazard Determination Form (FEMA Form 81–93), C146
Standard & Poor's, T128
Standards
   external audits, RM32–33
      fieldwork, RM33
      general, RM33
      reports, RM33
   generally accepted auditing standards (GAAS), RM34–35
   information systems, RM61–62
   risk-based audits, RM24–25
   See also Interagency Guidelines Establishing
State banks, RM6, RM11
State chartered institutions, COM170
State escheat laws, corporate trusts, T54
State nonmember banks, S20, S84–85
State regulations, RM11–12
State subdivision general obligations, COM140
Statutory veto power, over directors and executives, COM18
Stock bonus plans, T34
Stock exchange, C22–23
Stock margin, COM164
   bank, COM144–45, COM154
   See also Margin loans bank,
Stock registrar, T50–51
Stock transfer agent, T49–50
Stop payment, placed on checks, C115
Storage tanks, underground (USTs), COM88, COM90, COM93–95
Strategic-plan evaluation, C50, C53–54, C55
Strategic risk, RM15, RM18
Structuring of transactions, C30–31
Student Loan Marketing Association (Sallie Mae), COM140
Subaccounts, foreign bank, C28
Subordinated debt, COM53
Subscription agent, T52
Subsidiaries of listed corporations, C22
Subsidiary, foreign, COM117
Superfund Amendment and Reauthorization (SARA) (1986), T25
"Superfund" statute, COM88

Supervision by risk. *See* Risk-focused examination
Supervisory composite rating, COM77t
Supervisory oversight, RM8
Supervisory Release 96-10, T157
Supervisory Release 96-17, T99–100
Supervisory Release 97-17(GEN), T116
Supervisory Release 97-19, T88
Supplementary capital. *See* Tier II capital
Supreme Court, C37
Surety disclosures, C125
Surplus, definition of, COM133
"Surplus surplus" transfers, COM83
Suspicious Activity Report (SAR), C30, C38, COM33–34
    confidentiality of, COM36
    filing of forms, COM34–36
    mailing instructions, COM36
Suspicious transactions, reporting of, C30, C38
Swaps
    credit default, S40
    currency, S38
    interest rate, S38
    total rate of return (TROR), S40–41
Sweep programs, T81
S.W.I.F.T. system, C34, RM91
Syndicates, S89–90
Syndications, T111
Systems to Estimate Examination Ratings (SEER), RM122, RM174–75

T

"Tangible capital requirement," COM70
Target benefit plans, T34
Targeted population, C15
Tax Equity and Fiscal Responsibility Act (TEFRA) (1982), T42–43
Taxation
    charitable trusts, T20–21
    collective investment funds (CIFs), T126–27, T129, T135–36, T137, T138–39, T140–41
    corporate trusts, T50
    employee benefit/retirement plans, T32, T35, T42
    international trust services, T74–75
    portfolio management, T112–13
    trust by agreement, T20
Taxes, disclosure of (CLA), C61
Tax-exempt bond funds, T128
Taxpayer identification number (TIN), C41–42
Tax Reform Act (1976), T21
Tax Reform Act (1986), T42

TD F90-22-1 (FBAR), R16
Technology, RM7, RM60
Telecommunications, RM7
    in business recovery planning (BRP), RM89–90
    data integrity and, RM82
Temporary financing, C171
Tennessee Valley Authority, S17
Terminal receipt disclosures, C82
Termination, early, disclosure of (CLA), C60
"Terrorists, Specially Designated" (SDTs), COM101
Test library, RM71
TFR (OTS Form 1313), R33–35
Third parties
    brokerage operations, S58–59
    reporting and disclosure of, COM122
Third-party credit enhancements, COM50–51
Third-party evaluations and correspondents, COM105
Third-party research, T95
Thrift and savings plans, T34–35
Thrift Bulletin (OTS), COM67
Thrifts, capital categories and, COM72–73
Tier dividends, OTS, COM84–86
Tier I capital, COM12, COM50, COM54, COM133
    definition of, COM51–52
Tier II capital, COM12, COM50, COM133
    definition of, COM52–53
Tier III capital, COM68–69
Tier I leverage ratio, COM51
Tier I risk-based capital, 71t, COM70
Time account maturities, C228–29
Time deposits, COM192
    nonpersonal, COM193
Title companies, C179
Title VIII of the Civil Rights Act of 1968, C146
Title VII of the Civil Rights Act of 1964, C106–7
"Total Annual Loan Cost Rate" table, C219–20
Total capital, COM52
Total leverage capital, 71t, COM70
Total rate of return (TROR) swaps, S40–41
Total risk-based capital, 71t, COM70
Training, environmental risk program, COM95–96
Transaction accounts, definition of, COM192
Transaction identification, C204–5
Transaction risk, RM15
    audits and, RM22
    information systems and, RM54
Transfer agent
    for corporate trusts, T49–50
        turnaround performance requirements, T50

Index

Transfer agent *(continued)*
   mutual funds, S116-17
   shareholder services and, T58–60
      for mutual funds, T61–62
      registration of, T62
Transfer of funds. *See* Funds transfer rules
Transfer risk, COM121
Transportation of currency and monetary instruments (CMIR), C37–38
Travel rule. *See* Payment order information (travel rule)
Treasury Department. *See* U.S. Department of Treasury
"Troubled" condition of financial institutions, COM18
Trust access limitations, T85
Trust Banking Circular
   No. 19, T111
   No. 23, T112
Trust by agreement, T19–20
Trust by declaration, T19–20
Trust department operations
   accounting control, T78–80
   accounting reconcilement, T80
   Bank Secrecy Act (1970), T87–88
   cash accounts, T80–81
   cash overdrafts, T81–82
   dividend/income claims, T83
   free-riding, T93–94
   institutional delivery/settlement, T96
   money laundering, T88
   nominee registration, T84
   pledge requirements, T82
   principal/income separation, T80
   purpose of, T78
   references regarding, T100
   safekeeping
      dual control, T85
      duty separation, T85
      limited trust access, T85
      off-premise custody, T86
      on-premise custody, T84–85
      piggyback arrangement, T86, T96
      U.S. government securities, T86–87
      vault protection, T85
   securities income processing, T82–83
   securities lending, T96–99
      borrower credit analysis, T97
      cash collateral, T98
      collateral margins, T97–98
      lending agreement, T97
      letters of credit, T99

Trust department operations *(continued)*
      securities collateral, T98–99
   securities trade processing, T88–91
      best execution, T89, T94
      quarterly reports, T92–93
      trade confirmation, T91–92
      trade execution, T90–91
      trade orders, T89–90
      trade policies/procedures, T92
   shareholder communications, T99
   soft dollars
      directed brokerage, T95–96
      safe harbor, T94–95
      third-party research, T95
   sweep programs, T81
   trust disbursements, T83–84
   year 2000 preparedness, T99–100
Trust disbursements, T83–84
Trust Indenture Act (1939), T53, T54
Trust Interpretive Letter
   Number 217, T120
   Number 234, T121
   Number 235, T120
   Number 273, T112
   Number 525, T121
Trust Regulatory Handbook, The, C3
Trust-related accounts, insurance coverage of, C76
Trust services
   international
      foreign trusts, T74–75
      laws/regulations for, T74
      purpose of, T74
      references regarding, T75
   pricing for, T11–12
   See also Corporate trusts; Employee benefit/retirement plans; Personal trusts; Shareholder services
Trust under will, T19
Truth in Lending Act (TILA)
   amendment to, C4, C191
   closed-end credit. *See* Closed-end credit
   consumer credit, C192
   credit categories, C193
   disclosures. *See* Truth in Lending Act (TILA) disclosures
   exempt transactions, C192–93
   home equity lines of credit (HELCs), C174, C209–12
   introduction and purpose, C191
   issuance of access devices, C81
   issuance of credit cards, C201
   laws and regulations references, C222

46 Compliance Link

Truth in Lending Act (TILA) *(continued)*
   open-end credit. *See* Open-end credit
   scope of, C191–92
   subsequent events, C194
Truth in Lending Act (TILA) disclosures, C193–94
   annual percentage rate (APR), C194, C195–96
   annual percentage rate (APR) accuracy tolerances, C196–97
   application, C201–2
   calculations and estimates, C194
   closed-end credit. *See* Closed-end credit disclosures
   finance charge, C193, C194, C195, C196, C197–200, C221
   maximum interest rates (ARM), C10
   multiple creditors or consumers, C195
   open-end credit. *See* Open-end credit disclosures
   refinancing, C194–95
   required, C193–94
Truth in Savings Act (TISA)
   account disclosure, C224–29
   advertising, C167, C230–31
   civil liability, C231
   covered accounts, C224
   distribution of disclosures, C227–29
   interest payment, C229
   interim rule amending Regulation DD, C226–27
   introduction and purpose, C224
   laws and regulations references, C231
   periodic statements, C229
Turnaround performance requirements
   for corporate trusts, T50
   shareholder services and, T63–66
     business expansion limitations, T64
     exemptions, T65
     recordkeeping, T66
     written inquiry turnaround, T65
Tutor, T22
Two-day/four-day test, C121
Tying provisions
   exceptions, COM199
   introduction and purpose, COM198
   laws and regulations references, COM200
   private lawsuits, COM199
   prohibited arrangements, COM198–99
Type III securities, S7, S16, S18, S76
Type II securities, S7, S16, S17–18, S76
Type I securities, S7, S16, S17, S18, S76
Type IV securities, S16, S18, S76
Type V securities, S16, S18–19, S76

U

Unauthorized loans, insiders and, COM152
Undercapitalized institutions, COM38–39, COM49, COM71–72
Underground storage tanks (USTs), COM88, COM90, COM93–95
Underwriter, purchase from affiliate as, COM15
Underwriting
   credit, COM6
   nondiscrimination in, C138
Underwriting/dealing activities, Government Securities Act (GSA) (1986)
   dealing defined, S77
   dealing vs. trading, S77
   Glass-Steagall Act and, S6–8, S18, S19, S76–84
   Government Securities Act (GSA) (1986)
     broker-dealer registration, S99–100
     exemptions, S100–101
     hold-in-custody repurchase agreements, S23, S104–6
     overview of, S10, S99
     recordkeeping, S101–2
     safekeeping requirements, S102–4
     sales practices, S106–8
   Municipal Securities Rulemaking Board Regulations (MSRB), S86–98
     advertising, S94
     churning, S94
     confirmation requirements, S91–92
     control relationships, S94
     fair practice standards, S92–94
     financial advisory relationships, S94–95
     municipal securities principal, S87
     municipal securities representative, S87
     personnel qualifications, S87–88
     quotations, S91
     recordkeeping, S88–89
     sales/purchase reports, S91
     separately identifiable bank department, S86–87
     syndicates, S89–90
     uniform settlement practices, S90–91
   national bank operating subsidiaries, S84
   overseas, S121–22, S126–27
   references regarding, S83, S85, S98, S108
   Section 20 subsidiaries, S77–83
     adequate capital and, S79
     commercial paper and, S78
     consumer receivable-related securities and, S78

Index 47

Underwriting/dealing activities *(continued)*
 customer disclosure and, S80–81
 examinations for, S83
 foreign banks and, S82
 internal controls and, S79
 intra-day credit and, S81
 management restrictions and, S79–80
 mortgage-related securities and, S78
 municipal revenue bonds and, S78
 operating standards for, S79–83
 private placements and, S82
 purchase funding restrictions and, S81
 reporting requirements and, S81–82
 riskless principal transactions and, S82–83
 state nonmember bank subsidiaries, S84–85
 underwriting defined
  best efforts, S76–77
  firm commitment, S76
"Undivided profits," COM82–83
Unemployment, and distressed community, C14
Unenforceable loans, COM140
Uniform Bank Surveillance Screen (UBSS), RM175
Uniform Commercial Code, C31, T28
Uniform Commercial Code Article 4A (UCC4A), RM91–92
Uniform Common Trust Fund statutes, T139
Uniform Financial Institutions Rating System (UFIRS) (CAMELS), COM18, RM122, RM125–37
 asset quality, RM128, RM129–30
 CAMELS acronym, RM128
 capital adequacy, RM128, RM129
 earnings, RM128, RM132–33
 FDICIA connection, RM136–37
 liquidity, RM128, RM133–34
 management/administration, RM128, RM130–32
 market risk sensitivity, RM128, RM134–36
 overview of, RM125–27
 performance evaluation, RM128–36
Uniform Gifts to Minors Act, C74, T28, T127
Uniform Interagency Rating System/Data Processing Organizations, RM122, RM170–74
 audits, RM171
 computer operations, RM174
 management, RM172–73
 systems/programming, RM173
Uniform Interagency Trust Rating System (UITRS), RM122, RM137–46, T155, T156, T157
 account administration, RM141–42
 asset administration, RM140–41

Uniform Interagency Trust Rating System *(continued)*
 conflict of interest, RM142–43
 earnings/volume trends/prospects, RM143–45
 operations/controls/audits, RM139–40
 proposed changes for, RM145–46
 supervision/organization, RM138–39
Uniform Principal and Income Act, T28, T80
Uniform Probate Code, T28
Uniform Settlement Statement (HUD-1 and HUD-1A), C174–75
Uniform Simultaneous Death Act, T28
Uniform Trust Fund Act, T28
Uniform Trust Powers Act, T28
"Unimpaired capital and surplus," COM151
Unqualified report, RM34
Unsecured loans, COM132, COM175
U.S. Attorney General, C103
U.S. Criminal Code, C37, C184
U.S. Customs Office, COM102
U.S. Customs Service, C37, C38
 CMIR (Form 4790), R15
U.S. Department of Housing and Urban Development (HUD)
 Fair Housing Act and, C136, C137
 home-ownership counseling and, C160-61
 Housing and Urban Development Act of 1968, C160
 HUD-1 and HUD-1A, C172, C173, C174–75
 Mutual Mortgage Insurance Fund, C161
 See also Real Estate Settlement Procedures Act (RESPA)
U.S. Department of Justice (DOJ), C93, C136
U.S. Department of Labor, C106, C108, C109, S28, T37, T38, T112, T121–22, T140
U.S. Department of the Treasury, C20, C33, C35
 checks, C113
 Financial Crimes Enforcement Network (FinCEN), COM36
 Office of Foreign Assets Control (OFAC), COM100–102
U.S. Department of Veterans Affairs, C161
U.S. foreign policy, COM100
U.S. General Accounting Office (GAO), C185
U.S. government securities, T86–87
U.S. obligations, loans secured by, COM139
U.S. Postal Service, money orders, C113
U.S. Secret Service
 Financial Crimes Division, COM36
 Form S, R114
 SSF 1604, R52
U.S. Supreme Court, C37

V

Value-at-risk (VAR), COM68, COM69
Variable rate information, C203, C210
　　disclosures, 203, C210
Vault cash, COM195
Vault protection, T85
Veterans Administration (VA), C155
　　mortgage insurance, C145
Veterans Affairs, Department of, C161
Veterans Employment Service, C109
Veto power, over directors and executives, COM18
Vietnam Era Veterans Readjustment Act of 1974, C109

W

Wages. *See* Earnings
Waivers
　　brokered deposits, COM40
　　capital exposure limit, COM107
　　credit practice rules and, C66, C67
Warranties, disclosure of (CLA), C60
"Warrant of attorney," C66
Watch lists, S73
Well-capitalized institutions, COM38–39, COM49, COM71, COM73
"When issued" securities trading, S32
When Your Home Is on the Line: What You Should Know about Home Equity Lines of Credit, C172–73
Whole sale purpose institutions, community development test, C52–53
Wire transfers, C33–34
Wire transfer systems, COM76
Work-out activities, secured creditor exemption for UST, COM95
World Bank, S17

Written agreements, securities lending, S27
Written policies/procedures, derivatives, S45

X

X-17F-1A, R49–50

Y

Y-9C Report, COM68
Year 2000 preparedness, T99–100
Year 2000 problem, operational issues
　　board of director responsibility, RM112–13
　　certification requirements, RM116–18
　　consumer issues, RM111
　　contracts, RM119
　　external risks, RM111
　　　　corporate customers, RM118
　　　　data exchange, RM118
　　　　vendor relations, RM118
　　foreign banks and, RM111
　　industry coordination, RM118
　　mergers/acquisitions, RM119
　　overview of, RM110
　　project assessment, RM114
　　project guidelines, RM115–16
　　project on-site examination, RM114–15
　　project planning, RM113–14
　　　　replacement vs. repair, RM119
　　　　special dates, RM119
　　supervisory follow-up for, RM111–12
　　Y2K timeline for, RM110, RM117–18

Z

Zero cap, COM79
Zion National Bank, S84